# Language, experience
# and school

Explorations in Language Study
*General Editors:*
Peter Doughty   Geoffrey Thornton

# LANGUAGE, EXPERIENCE AND SCHOOL

## Geoffrey Thornton

**EDWARD ARNOLD**

© Geoffrey Thornton 1974

First published 1974
by Edward Arnold (Publishers) Ltd.
25 Hill Street,
London W1X 8LL

ISBN: 0 7131 1887 3

## Already published in this series

Language in the Junior School
E. Ashworth

Language and Community
E. A. and P. S. Doughty

Language Study, the Teacher and the Learner
P. S. Doughty and G. M. Thornton

Language, Brain and Interactive Processes
R. S. Gurney

Explorations in the Functions of Language
M. A. K. Halliday

Learning How to Mean:
Explorations in the Development of Language
M. A. K. Halliday

English as a Second and Foreign Language
B. Harrison

Language in Bilingual Communities
D. Sharp

Printed in Great Britain by Butler & Tanner Ltd.,
Frome and London

# General Introduction

In the course of our efforts to develop a linguistic focus for work in English language, now published as 'Language in Use', we came to realise the extent of the growing interest in what we would call a linguistic approach to language. Lecturers in Colleges and Departments of Education see the relevance of such an approach in the education of teachers. Many teachers in schools and in colleges of Further Education see themselves that 'Educational failure is primarily linguistic failure', and have turned to Linguistic Science for some kind of exploration and practical guidance. Many of those now exploring the problems of relationships, community or society from a sociological or psychological point of view wish to make use of a linguistic approach to the language in so far as it is relevant to those problems.

We were conscious of the wide divergence between the aims of the linguist, primarily interested in language as a system for organising 'meanings', and the needs of those who now wanted to gain access to the insights that resulted from that interest. In particular, we were aware of the wide gap that separated the literature of academic Linguistics from the majority of those who wished to find out what Linguistic Science might have to say about language and the use of language.

Out of this experience emerged our own view of that much-used term, 'Language Study', developed initially in the chapters of 'Exploring Language', and now given expression in this series. Language Study is not a subject but a process, which is why the series is to be called 'Explorations in Language Study'. Each exploration is focused upon a meeting point between the insights of Linguistic Science, often in conjunction with other social sciences, and the linguistic questions raised by the study of a particular aspect of individual behaviour or human society.

5

Initially, the volumes in this series have a particular relevance to the role of language in teaching and learning. The editors intend that they should make a basic contribution to the literature of Language Study, doing justice equally to the findings of the academic disciplines involved and the practical needs of those who now want to take a linguistic view of their own particular problems of language and the use of language.

Peter Doughty
Geoffrey Thornton

# Contents

# Acknowledgements

I am grateful to those who have helped, in various ways, with the writing of the book, especially Eric Ashworth and Peter Doughty, Stephen Lushington and Frank Skitt. The responsibility for where the argument leads is mine.

Geoffrey Thornton

# Introduction

Most teachers would agree that a fair proportion of the discussion in educational circles at the present time is concerned with the idea of 'the pupil's needs', and these 'needs' are usually discussed in terms of how the curriculum, and the teaching which implements it, can best meet them. Now this is a very important change of focus, a change which asks every teacher to ensure that what he teaches, and how he teaches it, always relates to the pupil who has to do the learning rather than the subject which has to be taught. There is a very important aspect of 'the pupil's needs', however, which has been somewhat overlooked—the pupil 'needs' teachers who are aware of *all* the factors which can influence the effectiveness of his learning. He needs teachers who are as aware of the part played by the life of the school as they are of the part played by the syllabus of a subject, or the dictates of an examination, in shaping how and what can be learnt. He needs teachers who are as conscious of the *process* of learning, and its critical medium, language, as they are of the *content* of what they teach and its potential relevance to the lives of their pupils.

If such needs as these on the part of the pupil are to be satisfied, however, teachers in their turn will have new needs. It is not enough to 'know your subject', or even, how best to 'put it over'. There is no sadder sight at the present time than the prospect of a well-informed and professionally very capable teacher slowly turning from enthusiasm to dismay, and then to disillusion, because all his best efforts have come to nothing, defeated, not by his choice of what to teach, or by his inability to teach it, but by his unawareness. He has not seen that there are features of the school community in which he works, the boundaries it sets up, or its 'message systems', or its attitudes to learning, or to language for learning, which have come between him and his pupils. Geoffrey

9

Thornton has taken this situation as his basic theme for *Language, Experience and School*. He sets out to show every teacher that the way the life of a school is organised, the way it has come to function as an autonomous community, setting its own goals, writing its own laws, and inventing its own patterns of social behaviour, is decisive in determining how successfully teaching and learning can take place within it.

A reader may wonder at this point why such a book should appear in a series called *Explorations in Language Study*. The answer is simple. Just as language is the crucial means by which we create human communities, so language is the decisive factor in creating the life of the school community. For this reason, Geoffrey Thornton begins by looking at the way we learn language before he goes on to describe how language functions in the context of the school. He wants the reader to have before him at each stage the clear sense that every pupil already knows how to use language as a member of a human community before ever he enters school. As he says, however, 'Schools are *communities* which exist to promote learning'. The school does in little what is done by the larger community outside. It uses language to promote, maintain and regulate relationships. It uses language to create and transmit values. It uses language as a major means for conveying information of all kinds. For the majority of teachers, however, 'language' in school is only what is used for conveying that particular form of information they call 'knowledge' backwards and forwards between teacher and pupil.

Throughout this book, Geoffrey Thornton asks the teacher to focus upon all those other ways of using language that go on in school, and to consider how they form a single pattern of interrelated 'message systems', the function of which is to give the school its own social and cultural identity. He points out that some of the most important of these 'message systems', like rules about dress or social behaviour, reveal an intimate interrelationship between verbal and non-verbal ways of conveying meanings. Perhaps as a result of their continuous preoccupation with the language of intellectual processes, teachers are often inclined to overlook the importance of message systems that are not wholly verbal, but it is just these systems which create the collective social and cultural life of the school community. For this reason, Geoffrey Thornton argues that a teacher should always be aware of three major aspects of the language activity of his school community: (1) how language is used as a 'pure' medium in relation to intellectual processes; (2) how language is used as a 'mixed' medium to give the school its social and cultural identity; (3) what effect the school's 'mixed' message systems may have upon the use of language for learning in the context of his own classroom.

These three aspects, taken together, vitally affect the success or failure of the school's central function, the promotion of learning. There is yet another factor, however, which has just as vital an effect upon this success or failure. Geoffrey Thornton points out that the pupil comes to school already possessing a highly developed experience of language, an experience intimately bound up with his knowledge of the message systems of his own community. Given the present nature of our society, the school's view of its function, and the teacher's view of his role, what this means in so many cases is a head-on clash between the pupil's experience of language for living and the school's attitude to language for learning.

In Chapter 5, he shows how the clash between the language habits of the home community and the school community's attitudes towards language can have so disastrous an effect upon the climate for language activity in the class room. In Chapter 6, he goes on to take a close look at what is demanded of pupils in terms of language for learning. In particular, he examines five examples of what the school regards as appropriate language for learning and shows how they present the ordinary pupil with the equivalent of a complex and difficult 'language game' for which he has not been given the rules. Finally, in Chapter 8, he gives a most thought-provoking analysis of one effort one particular student made to bridge the gap between the language she could use so successfully as a member of her home community and the language demanded of her by the context for learning she had been placed in. What this example demonstrates so admirably is the need for every teacher to ask himself how far his own school community promotes a language climate favourable to learning and how far it inhibits, or actively discourages, the pupil from using in school the only language he has, the language of his home community. The aim of this book is to help the teacher to do this successfully.

PETER DOUGHTY

# 1 Language in school

There is a haunting remark in a paper by Bernstein, called 'Social Class, language and socialisation', where he says,

'. . . differently-focused experience may be disvalued and humiliated within schools, or seen, at best, to be irrelevant to the educational endeavour.'[1]

There is a passage in Halliday's *Language and Social Man* which contains more than an echo of this:

'. . . but as things are, certain ways of organising experience through language, and of participating and interacting with people and things, are necessary to success in school. The child who is not disposed to this type of verbal exploration in this type of experiential and interpersonal context 'is not at home in the educational world', as Bernstein puts it. Whether he is so predisposed or not turns out not to be any innate property of the child as an individual, an inherent limitation on his mental powers, as used to be generally thought; it is merely the result of a mismatch between his own symbolic orders of meaning and those of the school. . . .'[2]

And in a paper called, 'Code, Register and Social Dialect', Ruqaiya Hasan makes this point:

'educational failure may not be as much a result of the pupil's inability to master the concepts as that of the educational system which fails to establish any relevance between these concepts and the pupil's living of life, especially where the life in the school is not a simple extension of life outside.'[3]

These quotations express a common concern with problems of educational success and failure, while the writers share a conviction that explanations of success and failure are to be sought, ultimately, in the inability of the school system always to enable

13

the pupil to make the best use of his basic resource for learning, his language. They suggest, in other words, that 'as things are', some pupils enter school predisposed to success while some enter it predisposed to failure.

It is the intention of this book to explore the basis of this contention; and to ask how it comes about that schools can be charged with discounting as 'irrelevant to the educational endeavour' the experience of language and life (the only experience that they could have had!) that some pupils bring into school with them. This entails looking for the factors which make for educational success or failure in the relationship that is set up between school and pupil, and asking why it is that some kinds of relationship point the pupil towards failure and some towards success.

This will involve setting up an opposition between the pupil, an individual human being with a capacity for using language, and the school, an institution which, by its very nature, exists to make constant, quite special, demands on the languaging capacity of its pupils.

The focus of the exploration will be language, language conceived as something that was evolved for *use* in the furtherance of the daily communion with other people of which life consists. We learn language through growing up in a human community. We go on using language throughout the rest of our lives in the process of establishing and maintaining relationships in community with other people. We learn language through contact with other people, we use language in contact with other people, and we make a mistake if we regard language as something that can be divorced from the situation in which it is used, and the purpose for which it is used in that situation.

Language is social. Within a social context, language has purpose and point; it is functional. And its function is to enable human beings to exchange meanings with each other. Language is for meaning.

As human beings, most of us learn that this is so during the early years of life, when we acquire an ability to put into language a range of meanings adequate to our needs. Most children enter school with an already well-developed potential for language, yet—as pupils in school—many of them quickly find that they are unable to meet the language demands that school makes upon them in a way that the school regards as adequate.

This book is not intended to be another contribution to the

discussion about the relationship between language, social class and educability. Nor is it intended as a formulation of another 'deprivation theory', whether social or linguistic. The effect of all explanations of educational failure based upon a notion of the pupil's deprivation, of whatever kind it is thought to be, is to place the onus of failure, ultimately, on the shortcomings of the pupil himself, and therefore to absolve the school from its responsibility.

It is the school which constructs the context in which the pupil succeeds or fails, which creates the conditions under which the pupil will, or will not be able, to exploit the potential that he comes into school endowed with—his language and experience, and his own amalgam of knowledge, interests and abilities. It is the school which has the responsibility of matching the contribution brought to the learning situation by the pupil, of—in the old phrase—'starting where the pupil is'. In fact, you can't start anywhere else.

If this is to mean anything at all, it means starting where the pupil is in terms of his own language, and, for this to be done, there must be, on the part of the teacher, a real understanding of what language is, and how it works, so that he may recognise the pupil's linguistic potential for what it really is, and know how to tap it.

This means understanding that language is social and functional, and recognising that the school is a community in which the pupil is also a person. The demands which the school makes on him as a pupil are also made upon him as a person. The way in which he can respond to those demands is determined not only by the nature of the demands themselves but also by the position he is put in to respond to them. The position, that is, that the school has put him in. A school is not merely a collection of individual pupils responding to the demands of learning situations. It is a community in which people, teachers and pupils, live part of their lives, and life inside the school is as real as life outside, not least because the relationships within the school are real. And it is the nature of the relationships that determines the way in which people within the school, teachers and pupils alike, can behave, and perform, succeed and fail.

This means that any search for explanations of why pupils succeed or fail must look at the relationships set up between pupil and teacher, and at what each brings to the relationship.

Chapter 2 will start by looking at the language which a pupil brings. It will discuss initial language acquisition as a process whereby what is acquired is the ability to make meanings in language. The question to be asked is, 'What has the child learnt to do with language by the time he arrives in school?'

In order to begin to answer the question, 'What can he do with his language in school?' Chapters 3 and 4 will look at the nature of the school as a community, and the place of the pupil within it, while Chapter 5 will examine attitudes to language prevalent in school. Chapter 6 will look at the kind of demand typically made upon pupils' language in school, and Chapter 7 will ask what opportunities pupils are normally given to develop the ability to meet them.

The final chapter, asking 'What is to be done?', argues the need for all teaching to be informed by an adequate and relevant knowledge of the nature and function of language as a first step towards achieving a situation in which some pupils need no longer enter school already heading for failure.

# 2 Language and meaning

'Looking at the early stages of language development from a functional viewpoint, we can follow the process whereby the child gradually "learns how to mean", for that is what first-language learning is. If there is anything which the child can be said to be "acquiring", it is a range of potential, which we could refer to as his "meaning potential".'

*Language and Social Man*—M. A. K. Halliday

## The process of language learning: 'learning how to mean'

Human beings are, with few exceptions, born into the world with a brain that has the potential to learn language. Individual human beings are born into a community where spoken language is in constant use between the people who make up that community. The language that each individual acquires will be the language of that community, which he learns for himself as he experiences language while growing up.

The individual has, in other words, a potential for learning language physically located in his brain, and this potential is realised by the language which he hears in use around him. The process is one whereby an *individual*'s potential is realised by a *communal* act or, rather, an unending succession of communal acts, as language enters into the transactions of daily life around him.[4]

Man evolved language in order to convey meaning. To make meaning with language, the sounds and words of which it is composed have to be combined in ways that other people can understand. We can say, with J. R. Firth, that the 'elements' of which language is composed have to be put together into 'structures'. Another way of viewing the process is to regard language as having three levels, levels of sounds, of words, and of meanings. Sounds are organised into words, and words put together in order to make meanings.

This, however, is only a rough outline of what happens. At the level of sounds, there is much more involved than the sounds themselves. There are all the features of spoken language, features such as intonation, stress, and the kind of pause which makes 'I scream' mean something different from 'ice-cream'. When the level of sounds is referred to, in linguistics, as the level of *phonology*, it is taken to include all these features of spoken language which may be used to make the meaning of one utterance different from another.

At the level of words, it is necessary to remind ourselves that words have to be organised and combined into larger stretches of language if they are to carry meaning. How words are put together in a language constitutes the grammar of the language. Thus, the level of words is more properly the level of words and grammar, or the lexico-grammatical level. The phonological and lexico-grammatical levels exist in order that we can make meaning with language. That is, they exist for the sake of the third level, the level of meaning.

In a well-known paper, 'Relevant Models of Language', M. A. K. Halliday suggested that an individual learns for himself, in infancy, that the function of language is to make meanings by encountering, and experiencing for himself, language used for at least seven different purposes. These he called the Instrumental ('I want') purpose, the Regulatory ('do as I tell you'), the Heuristic ('tell me why'), the Imaginative ('let's pretend'), the Interactional ('me and you'), the Personal ('here I am'), and the Informative ('I've got something to tell you').

Using these as the basis of his observation, Halliday subsequently observed, and described as a process whereby what is learnt is how to make meanings, the language development of a child in the first years of its life. He shows how, in the case of the infant under observation, 'early vocal sounds, although still pre-linguistic in the sense that they were not modelled on the English language, were used effectively for just these purposes—to obtain goods and services that he required (instrumental), to influence the behaviour of those closest to him (regulatory), to maintain his emotional ties with them (interactional) and so on. The meanings that he can express at this stage—the number of things that he can ask for, for example—are naturally very restricted, but he has internalised the fact that language serves these purposes.'[2]

The child learns very early in life what language is for. Indeed, Halliday notes that, by the age of 18 months, the child 'could use language effectively in the instrumental, regulatory, interactional and personal functions, and was beginning to use it for pretend-play (the imaginative function) and also heuristically, for the purpose of exploring the environment', that is, for six out of seven functions. The informative function is the last to be mastered, for reasons which will be discussed later.

Looked at from this 'functional viewpoint', that is from the viewpoint of seeing language as something that is used for practical purposes, Halliday can claim that, 'By the age of two and a half or even earlier', the child has laid the foundations for his subsequent mastery of language. 'The framework is all there.'

Because it sees language learning as being essentially a process of learning how to make meanings in language, this is a strikingly different account of the first stages of language learning from that which is commonly held. Popular beliefs about early language learning, beliefs of the kind described in *Exploring Language*[5] as 'folk-linguistic notions of language', centre around the tendency to equate language with words. The utterance of a child's first word is normally hailed as the first step along the road of linguistic development. But by the time the child utters his first recognisably word-like combination of sounds, he has already travelled some distance along the road. He has already taught himself how to structure sounds and intonations into ways of making meanings.

He has not only grasped, intuitively, the fact that language is for making meanings with but is able to exploit the phonological level for this purpose before he develops the ability to exploit the lexico-grammatical level as well. It is worth noting, because the point will have to be considered later, that this intuitive grasp of the nature and function of language that a child displays early in life normally becomes overlaid, later on, with culturally taught 'folk-linguistic notions' of language. There persist in our culture deep-rooted misconceptions about language, which are transmitted from generation to generation, despite the penetrating insights into language made available by linguists in the last thirty years and despite the obvious fact that the way in which language is used in the course of our daily lives is completely at variance with the way in which most adults seem to think it is used.

By the age of about three, any normal child will have mastered the sounds of the language in use around him, and will already be able to put together basic lexico-grammatical structures. Thus early in life, he will have laid the foundations of his langage.

He will also be learning that language is not the only method by which human beings communicate, that is share meanings, with each other, although it so happens that language is the most complex and subtle system so far evolved for the purpose. Communication between people, at least in face-to-face situations, takes place in ways which involve exploiting bodily features in systematic ways. Facial expressions, bodily postures and gestures all play their part in the process of exchanging meanings. Although it is convenient, as in a book like this, to distinguish between verbal and nonverbal communication, it is important to remember that when two human beings are communicating in a face-to-face situation they are using verbal and nonverbal means interdependently. The expression which accompanies 'Are you coming?' will help to determine whether what has been said means a question, a command, or a threat. The length of the silence before an answering 'No' may convey as much meaning as the 'No' itself.

'When we study communication as the process by means of which people relate to each other, we must look at the context in which it occurs—the human relationship. And when we examine a human relationship, such as a simple conversation between two people, we almost immediately discover that there are multiple modalities or channels operating in addition to language. We discover that the modalities, verbal and nonverbal, are learned as patterns of the culture (as language is learned) and that they are systematic (as language has grammar, for example). Furthermore we discover that they all fit together: they are systematically interrelated.'
*Nonverbal Communication and the Education of Children*—Paul and
Happie Byers[6]

## The context of language learning

Language is learnt by the child from those around him as they use it in the course of their daily lives, but it is not learnt simply by a process of imitation. Such is the capacity of a human brain, that it can, during those early years of life, pick out the elements of language from the noise around it and teach itself how to put the elements together in structures that can convey meaning to others. It can take meaning from utterances that it has never heard before, and can put together structures that no one else has put together before.

Every child whose brain is thus developing the capacity to use language is a unique human being, at the centre of a unique network of relationships with other human beings. A number of factors will operate to ensure that this is so, factors such as sex, number in the family group, age of siblings already born, and so on. The son born as the eldest child will have a different relationship with his parents from his sister born a year or two later, while a boy born as the tenth child to a family already consisting of five girls and four boys will establish a pattern of relationships different from that already established by his brothers and sisters. And it is essentially in the course of establishing and maintaining those relationships that language is used in the life of day to day, as it is encountered by the child growing up. The relationships are the matrices within which language functions interdependently with the other means of communication mentioned in the last section. Who we are, and how we relate to the other person, determine what we want to mean, as a typical example of language in action will illustrate.

I go into a pub at lunch-time, and say to John behind the bar, 'Half of lager, please, and a cheese and onion jacket.' He takes a glass, puts it under the tap, turns the tap, and waits while the glass fills up. While he waits, we might exchange remarks about the weather, about the number of people in the bar, about the fact that I am alone when I am often with colleagues. If it is summer, and the television in the other bar is showing the Test Match, I might ask what the score is. I might, on the other hand, say nothing. It would not be considered odd if I did say nothing. In fact, John might, while he waited for the glass to fill, be carrying on a conversation with someone else.

When the glass is full, he puts it on the bar in front of me, and turns to the telephone at the end of the bar. He picks it up, and says, 'One cheese and onion jacket. Number six.' He puts the phone down, picks up a small plastic disc with the number 6 on it, and puts it on the bar in front of me, saying, 'Nineteen, please.' I offer him two tenpenny pieces, which he takes. He turns to the cash register, operates it, and turns back to me with a penny, which he hands to me. I put it in my pocket, pick up the plastic disc in one hand, the lager in the other, and turn to find a seat.

About five minutes later, the landlady comes in with a plate, on which is a potato that has been baked in its jacket, and cheese and onion added before it has been browned under the grill. It is a 'cheese and onion jacket'. She calls out, 'Number six.' I raise my hand, or call out something like, 'Over here.' She brings it across, puts it on the table, picks up the plastic disc, and says something. Invariably, she says something—about the weather, the number of people in the bar, the imminence of Race Day, something—before she goes to collect the order for 'Number seven'. Silence is, for her, not an option.

So a bit of language like 'cheese and onion jacket', not perhaps at first sight a lexico-grammatical structure likely to be meaningful, becomes meaningful in the social sequence in which it occurs, a social sequence in which people, and language, and actions, and things, interrelate. When I say, 'and a cheese and onion jacket', I know that the barman knows what I mean. When he says, 'Nineteen, please', he knows that, at that point in the sequence, I will understand him to mean that he is asking me for nineteen pence, the price of the lager and the cheese and onion jacket. It is a familiar routine, in which the interweaving of language with things and actions is taken for granted, just as the relationships of the participants in the scene are taken for granted.

Uses of language like this, asking for what we want, giving orders, fulfilling requests, maintaining friendly contact with people at work, are aspects of everyday living. What we say, and how we say it, in order to mean, is shaped by who we are talking to, the nature of our relationship with them, and when and why we are talking to them.

We begin the development of our own language by gradually becoming part of the everyday interchanges of life in a particular environment, the one into which we are born, where people have been habitually using language for a long time. The infant begins, tentatively, to encode meanings in sounds, and thus become part of new interchanges. He experiences which of the meanings get a response, and in what form, and builds such experiences into subsequent attempts to make meanings. At first, he encodes meanings in sounds, that is, only at the phonological level. In time, although it is, as we have seen, a comparatively short time, he develops the ability to use the lexico-grammatical level as well, and is ready to begin a career as an adult language user.

## Differing contexts of language learning

Halliday's 'Relevant Models' can be regarded as a description of the functional contexts within which language learning can take place. These functional contexts provide for the child the opportunity to learn (a) that language can be used for such and such a purpose, e.g. for getting what he wants, like a biscuit, and (b) the linguistic means of achieving his objective, e.g. 'bikky', 'bikky, please', or 'Can I have a biscuit?'

This way of looking at the language learning process provides us with a valuable way of comparing the differences which may exist, linguistically speaking, between environments in which children grow up.

Let us set side by side two extreme examples, which may be no more than ten geographical miles apart but which may be separated by a very wide social gulf. The first family consists of a teacher and his wife, herself a teacher before she married, and their three-year-old only son. The second family consists of a husband and wife, neither of whom can read and write, and three children under five, two boys and a girl. Both husband and wife work—he as a labourer, she as a cleaner.

We can, I think, fairly safely make a number of predictions about the amount and kind of language to which the teacher's son is exposed, compared with that which the youngest son of the labourer experiences. As the teacher's son begins to ask questions, it is probable that he will have them answered, not necessarily all the time, but frequently enough for him to grasp the notion that language is for asking questions and getting answers. (Halliday's heuristic model). Alone with his mother most of the day, he has no difficulty in realising that language is for talking to adults with. Doubtless his father will reinforce this realisation when he comes home, and, during the holidays, the way in which the boy is allowed, and encouraged, to talk to and with relatives and visitors, will also be a factor (Interactional). The way in which he is encouraged to play, by himself and with others, will influence his development of language for Imaginative purposes. By contrast, it is likely that the labourer's youngest son will be left in the company of his brother and sister for long periods. He will thus have less opportunity of talking to adults. He may, indeed, be positively discouraged from so doing, either because the parents are too busy, can't be bothered, or are simply not there. Questions may habitually go unanswered, so that the child

23

cannot come to appreciate the potential of language as a means of asking questions and getting answers. He cannot, therefore, develop his own potential. This doesn't mean that he can't, linguistically, construct a question ('Why . . .?'/'where . . .?'/ 'when . . .?'/'can't we . . .?'/'did he . . .?') but rather that he doesn't come to appreciate the possibilities of question and answer, because there is so little occasion in his life to experience the possibilities. We can take this contrast much deeper by looking closely at two more of the 'Relevant Models', the Personal and the Informative.

Who we are, and what the world is likely to have in store for us, is something that we learn, as we learn our language itself, from those around us. In fact, we learn these things largely in and through language itself. What it means to be a boy, or a girl, in a particular culture, or sub-culture, we learn by observing how men and women around us behave towards each other, and towards our brothers and sisters. We see what roles seem to be allocated to one sex or the other, what differences of dress and appearance distinguish one sex from the other, what is considered appropriate behaviour for each, how members of each sex talk about each other and about members of the opposite sex, and so on. The child comes eventually to see himself as a boy, or herself as a girl, and, on that foundation, to see his or her place in the world.

Dan Fader, the author of *Hooked on Books*,[7] once remarked that the only people who could afford to talk about the future were those who thought that they had a future. The future he meant was the kind predicated in statements like, 'I'm going to be a doctor', or 'I want to be an architect'. It is much more likely that the son of the teacher who is the subject of the comparison will, one day, make such a remark than will the girl who is the middle daughter of the illiterate labourer and his wife, and this for a number of reasons. An important one, of course, is that one is a boy, the other a girl—it is still much easier for a boy to become a doctor or an architect than for a girl. Another reason centres on the expectations of the parents: it is more than likely that the teacher and his wife will think in terms of a 'professional' career for their son. Another may have to do with the fact that the teacher's son is an only child, while the labourer's daughter is a second child. The son will inevitably spend more time in adult company, talking to and being talked to by adults. His exposure to adult concerns, and the language of adult concerns, is therefore

24

greater than that of a second (or third, or fourth) child, who will naturally spend time in the sole company of an elder brother or sister.

But the main point here is that, if there is, in the family, an anticipation that a child may be able to take a path towards a particular career, then it will be talked about—in all its aspects. And if it is talked about, the consequences for the child will be profound. He will come to realise that it is possible, indeed natural, to talk about such matters. He will have the opportunity of learning appropriate resources for talking about them, to hear and practice for himself language in which to discuss, probe, evaluate, and qualify. Language is thus playing its part in 'the process whereby the child becomes aware of himself', the process through which the child creates a self-image.

Another way of looking at what was going on when parents and child were discussing the future is to regard it as a process of exchanging information about the world. Halliday defined his Informative Model of language as the one which refers to 'the processes, persons, objects, abstractions, qualities, states and relations of the real world'.

It is the last of the seven 'Relevant Models' that the child learns how to function with, and this for a very significant reason. It makes more use of purely linguistic resources. It is language less bound to the context in which it occurs, language used to fashion abstractions and generalisations, language used in longer-than-usual stretches so that more sophisticated use has to be made of these linguistic devices which bind language together. (See p. 68.)

It is language use which needs experience and practice; language used to enable us to tell each other about what interests us, or is important to us, about what we think, or feel, or believe, about our understanding of the way the world is, and of the people in it. It is language used to discuss truth and beauty, right and wrong, the functioning of the international money market, or whatever, if we can language our meaning in such a way as to enable someone else to share it in a context which has made it possible.

Consider the following headline:

## OUR MIRAGE SHOULD FOIL IRISH GAMBLE

An essential clue to the meaning conveyed by the language is that the paper in which it appeared was a local sporting paper, published on Race Day. *Our Mirage* was the name of a horse, apparently fancied by the writer against an Irish entry regarded as something of a gamble. Those with sufficient knowledge of racing knew what he meant. They had access to the meaning which was being put into language, an access given by their experience of what is often called, aptly, the 'racing world', and its language.

A selection of the headlines appearing during the course of one week above the racing column in a national daily will emphasise the point.

CARSON GIVES HINT FOR GOLD COAST
PUNTERS PLUNGE AGAIN ON CAVO DORO
NEGUS HAS FINE CHANCE OF BIG DOUBLE
SNOWFIELD TO IMPROVE ON FIRST EFFORT
REALIST NAPPED TO RECOVER EBOR LOSSES

It is not simply a matter of knowing the names of jockeys (Carson), or horses (*Cavo Doro*), or understanding technical terms (napped, big double), or knowing that a horse called *Realist* had not run well in a race called the Ebor Handicap. It is a matter of knowing all this, and much more—of understanding the significance of the fact that Carson, the Champion Jockey, had chosen to ride a horse called *Gold Coast* when he could have chosen to ride another, of knowing what *Snowfield*'s 'first effort' had been, so that the significance of the opinion that it might be improved on might be properly estimated, and so on. When you know all this, you know what the language stands for, you know what it means.

Many people who go to France with the linguistic resource bequeathed by the French they learnt in school discover that they are able, more or less, to ask for a room, to order a meal, to buy petrol, ask the way, and engage in similar linguistic exchanges firmly wedded to a context, of reasonably short duration, and of fairly predictable outcome. They may even be able to hold a short conversation about the weather. But they are quite unable to sustain a discussion about the Common Market, the Channel Tunnel, or the Tour de France. They haven't the language, or the experience of language, necessary to encode their own meaning, or to gain access to somebody else's.

There are children who grow up without the opportunity to have abundant experience of language, especially the kind of language which constitutes the Informative Model. Whether
26

this is so or not will depend, essentially, on the number of adults in the family, and the use habitually made of language in the furtherance of the various relationships in the family.

There may be only one parent in the home, because of death, separation, or, temporarily, demands of a job which take the father away. Shift work, or handing over children to an *au pair* girl whose English is itself not very good, may lead to under-exposure to adult language, and thus a minimising of chances to experience and use it. Large numbers in a family may make for dilution of adult-generated and directed talk. And, over and above this, there must be taken into account habitual ways of using, or not using, language. 'Bugger off out of it', while meaning-ful, neither enhances the status of language as a form of com-munication nor affords opportunity to gain rich experience of language in the course of linguistic exchanges with other people.

There are children, on the other hand, who experience, as they grow up, language used by their parents, and perhaps other adults, for a variety of purposes. They hear all sorts of things being dis-cussed, and they themselves may be encouraged to participate. They thus learn that adults can be talked to and with about a multiplicity of things; they gain access to, and experience of using, the kinds of language in which things various can be talked about. Above all, they come to appreciate the possibilities of communicating in language, to see the power of language in enabling one to transcend the immediate context, to understand the potential of language for making meanings.

In this way, children acquire through experience their potential for making meaning in language, their 'meaning potential'. The process begins because the human brain can respond to the language heard in the environment, and the meaning potential initially acquired is intimately related to the environment in which it is acquired.

The process might, in fact, be described as one of acquiring a repertoire of meanings useful in the environment in which the child has grown up, intimately bound up with that environment, born out of the day-to-day exchange of meanings with those who people that environment, and the relationships he has with them. These meanings will be languaged in the habitual language of the environment—its phonology, its lexico-grammatical patterns— as the child makes it his own.

Each child might, then, be said to have his own, individual linguistic history, which will have endowed him with a linguistic

27

resource, a capacity for making meanings in language. This comprises not only his ability to put together the elements and structures of language at a given time, in response to a given situation, but also his knowledge about language—his intuitive knowledge of what language is for, of how and when to use it, and for what purpose.

But this resource is also a potential, for out of it he will draw what he can do with language in the future. Language learning, in the sense of being able to go on making more and more meanings in language, is a process that can go on throughout life. To what extent we can go on learning depends partly on the opportunities we get, and partly what we can make of them if we get them.

The child of five has learnt, with the opportunities that he has had, what he can do with language. Now he will have to learn what the school wants him to do with language. For some this will be easier than for others. Some will encounter obstacles that do not seem to appear in the way of others.

To begin to identify these obstacles it is necessary to look first at some aspects of the way in which the school functions as a community.

# 3  Schools as communities

'Only the Sixth Form may use the grass, the centre path and the path leading to the front door. The First Forms will use the path round the back, the Second Forms will use the path by the wall. Running on the paths is not allowed.'

Extract from School Rules

Schools are communities which exist to promote learning. It follows that, since language lies at the heart of nearly all learning, schools are communities which should allow, promote and encourage the use of language by the pupils for whose sake the schools exist.

Language is for use between people in social situations. For an individual wanting to use language (i.e. to make meaning) in a social situation, who and what he is, are, we have already insisted, factors which act upon his ability to draw upon his linguistic resource to make meaning. The small boy in the playground talking with two or three of his friends is in a very different situation from the small boy in the Head's study trying to explain why he threw glue at a small girl.

Life in school is an unending succession of situations calling for the use of language by people, both teachers and pupils, very conscious of their identity, of who and what they are, within the community. Schools are, in fact, very closely-knit communities which exert a fierce pressure on those who make up the community. Very conscious of its identity as this or that school, the school has a great capacity for making its members conscious of their own identities within it. This self-awareness is bound to be a powerful influence on opportunities for languaging meaning within the school.

29

## Boundaries

The establishing and maintaining of boundaries is a universal human need. We construct identities for ourselves, which we seek to protect. Against threats to identity we react vigorously. This leads us to mark out that bit of territory which we think of as ours, and defend it when we think it is being attacked. This is true at the individual level, when we think our jobs or our possessions or our beliefs are under attack, and it is true at the institutional level, when we defend the institutions in which we work against what we take to be a threat not only against their existence but also against what we see as making for order within the institution. Schools, and those who work in them, are no different, in this respect, from other institutions.

Schools which display a notice like PARENTS SHOULD NOT PROCEED BEYOND THIS POINT are, in effect, drawing a boundary across which they do not wish the parents of their pupils to penetrate. The Headmistress who wrote to a parent, 'We don't really encourage parents', was perhaps making the same point. The notice ALL VISITORS MUST REPORT TO THE OFFICE is defining a category—VISITORS—which is alien to the institution, and must, in case they should constitute a threat, be identified.

Within any institution there are people who are deeply concerned to see that its boundaries are maintained, since their own identities are heavily mortgaged in the institutions of which they are part.

The Head of a school sees himself as Head of that school. He has a conception of what being the Head of a school means, and has known this since he first realised that he wanted to be a Head and believed that he could do the job as he conceived it to be. He is thus bound up with his school, of whatever kind it happens to be: Infant, Junior, Primary; Secondary Modern, Comprehensive, Grammar, Bi-lateral; Middle, Upper, High, Sixth Form College; Boys, Girls or Mixed; Direct Grant or Independent; Aided or Controlled, whether Church of England, Roman Catholic or Jewish.

However, the Head is not the only one whose identity is bound up with the school. The whole staff is concerned, by virtue of their roles within the school. Most school staffs are arranged in hierarchies; the bigger the school the more elaborate the hierarchy. In small Primary Schools there will be a Deputy Head, with very little of a formal hierarchy beyond that created by age and experience, while in large Comprehensive Schools there will be a pyramid, with the Head at the top and, in rank order, various categories of staff—Deputy Heads, Senior Masters or Mistresses, Heads of Department, or Faculties, or Houses, or Years, various other posts of responsibility, and, at the bottom, young teachers and probationers.

Sooner, or later, any one of them will be concerned to maintain what he regards as a proper boundary between what he sees as his role in the school and that of any of his colleagues who may be thought to be trespassing.

Some such boundaries may be demarcated physically within the school-rooms set aside for the Head, the Deputy Head, the Reception Class, the Library, the Science Department, and so on. These areas become territories to be defended, so much so that the Science Department in one school was known, to both staff and pupils, as 'The Kremlin', because no members of staff other than members of the Science Department went in.

But boundaries may be erected in much more subtle ways than this. There is the claim to performance of certain duties ('that's my job'), possession of things ('that's my peg/chair/mug'), wearing of special clothing, such as gowns, track-suits or lab coats. At one school, there used to be two 'tea-clubs' within one department, one for graduates and one for non-graduates, while in another students on teaching practice were relegated to a stock cupboard to take their morning break. By such strategies as these, strategies which are regrettably absorbed into the routine of living, boundaries are set up and maintained, and there will inevitably come times in the life of every member of staff when they find themselves vigorously defending what they regard as their boundaries against what they conceive to be a threat.

New members of staff, especially those who join a school at junior level, have to learn to recognise boundaries, and to adjust their behaviour accordingly. They will soon, however, quickly learn not only to recognise boundaries but how to define their own. They will thus join the small army of boundary-maintainers of whom the school is composed. This is an inevitable process. A sense of stability is essential to life, and the existence of boundaries is an ingredient of stability.

Nevertheless, the way in which boundaries are set up and maintained within schools, the way in which members of staff regard certain boundaries as vital to their own sense of identity and react to defend them, will have a profound influence on the way in which the school behaves as a community. This, in turn, will act upon the way in which individuals in the school can behave as members of the community, and this, of course, includes linguistic behaviour—what we have the opportunity of meaning, and how, to whom and when. A probationer will soon learn, if he doesn't already know, the unwisdom of stopping the Head in the corridor, and saying 'By the way, I've been thinking about the way you do Assembly.' But in a Staff Meeting, where the subject of School Assembly has been put on the agenda, he (or she) is entitled to contribute to the discussion.

## Schools as message systems

The point was made in the last chapter that when two people communicate with each other, in a face-to-face situation, they make use of various ways, both verbal and nonverbal, of conveying meaning. Likewise, schools, as institutions, make use of a variety of ways of communication. These methods range from explicit, official, verbal messages to ways that are nonverbal, subtle, and unofficial, in the sense that they do not have behind them the full weight of the school's authority.

The school is, in effect, making use, all the time, of a multiplicity of message systems to convey meanings to pupils, meanings connected with daily routine, meanings connected with recurrent events in the school year, meanings which have to do with the existence and purpose of the school, and the behaviour of those in it. In one sense, the output of messages is random, in that they originate from many sources, from the Head downwards, in no particularly co-ordinated fashion. However, the effect of all this activity may be far from random, since its total impact may be such as to be clearly and unambiguously understood by pupils, although this impact may, in fact, be unappreciated by those in authority responsible for sending the messages, since they are not in a position to evaluate the relative effects of various kinds of message as their pupils are, and so measure the total impact. The emphasis placed on this message, or on that; the sanctions invoked to obtain compliance with this, or that rule; the public recognition given to this achievement, or that; the status afforded to this area of activity rather than that. All these add up, until, as might be said, the pupils *get the message.*

Perhaps the most explicit nonverbal system for conveying meaning is the bell, used to signal the beginning and end of school, or the whistle used to signal the beginning of school and the end of break or the lunch-hour. Schools vary in the forms of behaviour which they want linked to the sound of bell or whistle, and which they make verbally explicit, in lists of times posted in strategic places and/or in School Rules.

Pupils arriving after the First Bell will be registered as late.
Pupils must not be on the premises after the Last Bell unless engaged in an authorised activity.

School Rules appear to be the most explicit verbal statement of the school's meaning, but they tend to have an implicit meaning according to the seriousness with which they are taken, and the way in which they are enforced. Newcomers to a school have to learn not so much the rules themselves, but about the rules—which are thought important, and how they are enforced.

This can be illustrated with regard to school uniform. A Primary School sends out a notice to parents.

UNIFORM

*Boys* Grey shorts, grey shirt, School tie, grey pullover, black blazer, School cap.
*Girls* Grey skirt, white blouse, School tie, grey pullover. Cotton frocks are worn in summer.
Messrs. Freemantle, in the High Street, are the sole suppliers of School ties, badges, caps and berets.

The key question is, how is the wearing of school uniform encouraged? Is it compulsory, and if so how is the compulsion enforced? Would the school go to the lengths of asking a representative of Social Services to call on parents who said they couldn't afford school uniform and explain that a grant was available? If it is not compulsory, what strategies are used to suggest that the school regards the wearing of uniform as desirable? Is it only pupils who wear uniform who are given jobs of responsibility, or asked to show visitors around, or in any other way given public recognition? It is not necessary to have an explicit system of rewards and punishments to convey the school's approval or disapproval of certain forms of behaviour and certain kinds of achievement. It can be done in a number of subtle ways, although the full subtlety may not always be appreciated.

A boys' Grammar School, which reckoned to get 150 out of the 180 in any one entry up to O Level standard in four years, was faced with the problem of what to do with the remaining thirty. They couldn't go into the Sixth Form with their contemporaries, since they hadn't got the requisite number of O Levels, and therefore they couldn't wear Sixth Form uniform. The solution was to allow them what the school saw as the privilege of wearing Sixth Form blazers, but with bone instead of silver buttons. What the school didn't appreciate was that, since there were only thirty boys in the school wearing that particular uniform, and since what they had in common was their *failure* to achieve sufficient O Levels in four years to enter the Sixth Form, they were being distinguished, by their dress, as failures within the school.

Such distinctions between what the school regards as success and what it regards as failure can be made in other ways.

School magazines usually record achievements—sporting achievements, examination successes, distinctions won by former pupils. The way in which they are recorded is significant. The middle-page spread in a magazine from another Grammar School began with a list of scholarships and exhibitions to Oxford and Cambridge, continued with a note of those who had gained entrance to Oxford or Cambridge Colleges, and went on to those who had gained entrance (whether by scholarship or not) to other Universities. Then came a list of those who had gained places in other institutions of Higher Education, such as Polytechnics, Colleges of Advanced Technology and, at the end of the list, Colleges of Education. The school thus publicly stated a higher regard for the gaining of a place at Oxford or Cambridge than the winning of an entrance scholarship to another University.

The message is not lost on pupils, especially when it is reinforced by similar messages carried by other systems. Girls who have gone from Grammar School to Colleges of Education have testified to being made to feel second-rate within the school because they were not judged capable of aiming at University. Perhaps they were not in the top set, or doing subjects with the highest status, or in an Upper Sixth which had special privileges of accommodation, or were not considered first choices for positions of responsibility, or had to listen while enthusiasm was shown in Assembly for the success of those who had gained University places. In the end, the cumulative effect of such messages was clear: girls who were able enough to go on to Colleges of Education and become teachers themselves were made to feel second-rate within the community of their own school. There is little doubt that many of their teachers would be surprised and distressed to learn that the meaning of the school had been communicated so unambiguously to the pupils.

Every school sees itself as having a certain function to perform, and makes routine, regular and public declarations of its aims. Speech Days, Open Days, Open Evenings, Parents' Evenings, all such occasions afford opportunities to the school to explain what it thinks it is doing for its pupils, and why—small one-form-entry Primary Schools no less than twelve-form-entry Comprehensive Schools. But the way in which the school seeks to realise these aims in practice leads to the establishment of what is sometimes called 'the hidden curriculum', the strategies by which schools, like all institutions, as Berger and Luckmann put it in *The Social Construction of Reality*, 'by the very fact of their existence, control human conduct by setting up predefined patterns of conduct, which channel it in one direction as against the many other directions that would theoretically be possible.'[8]

This 'hidden curriculum' has the effect of enforcing a disposition towards certain forms of behaviour, and puts a premium on certain forms of achievement. Its specification remains implicit in the life of the community, its existence conveyed by an assortment of methods whose cumulative effect may be to press very hardly on those who have difficulty in decoding the messages, or who cannot meet its demands. There are those who pass the examination in the 'hidden curriculum', just as there are those who pass exams based upon more explicit criteria, and those who do not.

Those who do pass the test set by the 'hidden curriculum' are usually those whose cultural background is sufficiently close to that of the school to enable them to understand. Such pupils start their school life with an advantage that others do not have; they begin with a potential for success denied to others. And within the school context, it is success—success by the school's own criteria —that counts, success that is acclaimed.

One of the main arguments of this book is that, in any situation involving two or more human beings, who we are, and what we are, in that situation, has crucial consequences for what we can do in that situation, and that includes what we can mean. The status of pupils acclaimed as successful, as against those condemned as failures, is an important factor bearing upon the ability to perform in a given situation.

Among the messages most clearly received by pupils are those which tell them of their status within the community.

# 4   The making of a pupil

7) Pupils
         a) Dress and appearance
         b) Movement
         c) Pride in school
         Extract from agenda for Staff Meeting

Children enter the world of school for the first time, usually, at least in our society, at the age of five, to become pupils. They bring with them their own world, and a concept of themselves in that world. They bring with them, in other words, their own versions of reality, a version which they have constructed for themselves out of their experiences in the environment in which they grew up.

They enter the world of school, and meet people who have their own versions of reality, centred around their roles as teachers. And deeply embedded in these versions of reality are notions of normality and appropriacy regarding the behaviour of pupils, as pupils.

These notions may be no more than a loose congerie of expectations as to what are appropriate levels of performance. Such expectations are sometimes, especially in moments of stress, given expression in the admonition, 'You're not in the —— now', with the slot being filled by items like, 'Infants', 'Juniors', 'First Form', 'Fifth Form', and so on. The criteria on which the admonition is based are rarely made explicit. The teacher seemingly expects the pupil to know what is expected of him, appropriate to the point on the chronological-developmental scale he has reached. Pupils (presumably those who have been unable to discover the 'hidden curriculum') have been known to remark that, since they are never told what is expected of them as Juniors, or First Formers, or whatever, they feel that they can 'never win'.

The existence of these expectations is also implied in the perennial complaints that are heard—by Junior School teachers about what is not being done in the Infant Schools, by Secondary School Teachers about what is not being taught in Primary Schools, and by Lecturers in Universities and other institutions of Higher Education about what the schools are not doing. So successful does this kind of pressure become, that education tends to become a process whereby the pupil is merely prepared for the next stage. Educationalists are apt to talk about such things as 'The Needs of the Primary Child'. It would be more appropriate, perhaps, to talk about, 'What is needed to turn a child entering school into a Bottom Infant, then into a Middle Infant, a Top Infant, a Bottom Junior, and so on.'

## Pupils and knowledge

'. . . the form master must be firm and ensure that posters and pictures are always in the best taste and suitable for an academic atmosphere, i.e. not soccer heroes, lingerie advertisements, etc.'

Extract from School Rules

There is bound to be an initial gap, or mismatch, between John Smith, child, as he is when he enters school for the first time, and John Smith, pupil, as the school expects him to be.

Each child is an individual, who will come into school endowed with that mixture of abilities, interests and knowledge which growing up in a particular environment has allowed him to develop from his genetic potential. As Roger Gurney says in *Language, Brain and Interactive Processes*, 'The development of any organism provides ample evidence of the importance of interactive processes in producing the mature adult. In biological shorthand, we speak of the genotype (the individual genetic make-up) interacting with the environment to give the phenotype (the individual's personal characteristics). In short, $G \times E = P$, where $G$ is Genotype, $E$ is Environment and $P$ is Phenotype. The phenotype may be expressed in terms of height, hair colour, temperament, intelligence and so on, while the genotype consists of the genes controlling the development of these characteristics. Environment refers to any, or all, of the influences which bear upon the structure in question.'[9]

The gap will be partly that between what the school expects him to have in the way of knowledge when he comes in, and what knowledge he in fact possesses. The school may, on the one hand,

38

expect him to have certain knowledge which in fact he does not have, and, on the other hand, may not regard as legitimate, legitimate to the school context, knowledge which he does possess.

What *is* regarded as knowledge legitimate to the school context will depend partly on the teacher's own knowledge, and therefore his ability to appreciate, understand and share in the child's knowledge, and partly on what is traditionally regarded as educationally respectable.

At all levels, complaints can be heard.

'They don't know what —— is.'
'But he/she/they ought to know ——'

Perhaps, by certain criteria, they ought. But everybody's experience is limited, everybody's knowledge is partial. We all know something that somebody else doesn't; we are all ignorant of something that somebody else knows. We all, however, tend to think that what we know everybody else should know. This seems to be especially true in schools, however arbitrary the bit of knowledge is. But, if pupils don't know when it is thought they should, and if conditions are not provided in which they can come to know, then many will fail, ever, to close the gap between where they are, in terms of their own knowledge, and where their teachers think they ought to be.

This means, in fact, that, unless the school tries to close the gap by accepting the child for what he is, and for what he knows, and by providing him with an environment which will enable him to capitalise on the resources he brings with him into school, then as a pupil he starts his school career at a severe disadvantage. And if the school should start not merely by refusing to accept his knowledge for what it is but by devaluing what he brings into school, they will succeed only in devaluing him, thus virtually ensuring that the gap will never close.

The child whose background has endowed him with interests and knowledge that overlap with the concerns of the school has an obvious advantage over the child whose interests and knowledge are somewhat removed. Having access to the meaning of what is being discussed, the former is able to participate, and thus to capitalise on his language. The latter, unable to reach the language of the classroom, remains dumb. He is in an impossible position. What contribution he could make is likely to be, in Bernstein's word, 'disvalued', yet he is unable readily to share in the contributions made, with approval, by others. The seeds of

39

his failure have thus been sown by a system unable to make use of, or, more precisely, to allow him to make use of, what he possessed when he came into school. And the onus of failure is then normally thrown on the pupil, or on his background: social deprivation, or linguistic deprivation, or both, are invoked to explain the system's inability to provide for some the means to success that it provides for others.

Initial slowness in coming to terms with the concerns, the language, the meanings of the school may lead remorselessly to greater and greater failure, a process which seems to feed on itself, and which is clearly signalled to the pupil at every stage.

## Pupils and abilities

Of all the abilities that the child/pupil possesses, the most highly valued in school is what is called intellectual ability. Most of the labels hung on pupils reflect this: Able, Less Able, Very Able; High I.Q., Low I.Q., 'only an I.Q. of 110', and so on. It is not being argued that to place high value on intellectual ability is improper. For one thing, the development of people to their full intellectual capacity is not merely desirable in an advanced industrial society; it is a condition of survival. What is being argued is that when the regard for intellectual ability is enforced in such a way as to prevent the full realisation of the potential of those who do not appear to possess intellectual ability, this, apart from anything else, represents a gross under-use of talent.

Pupils in school operate, as pupils, within the framework provided by the school as a community. Exclusive regard for intellectual achievement has a damaging effect on the status within the school of those who appear to be incapable of such achievement, and we have already seen how message systems operate effectively to convey key meanings within the school. Yet the criteria used to estimate intellectual ability are often grossly inadequate.

Judgment is based, roughly speaking, on the way in which pupils respond to the demands made upon them in school, how quickly and, in the eyes of the teacher, how successfully. From achievements, judgments are made about the capacity which is presumed to underlie those achievements. And to reinforce 'subjective' judgments, so-called 'objective' tests are called upon. We shall see in the next chapter how misconceptions about pupils' language can issue in mistaken judgments about their intellectual potential, but it is worth noting here that tests designed to measure intelligence are themselves not free from the same sort of confusion, since they are, in the main, still based upon inadequate ideas of the way in which language actually works.

For one thing, they ignore what we know about the effect of the context itself upon ability to use language in that context. Tests are often administered under conditions calculated to induce anxiety, especially in pupils who have already been convinced of their inadequacy, so that results obtained cannot be other than misleading. Indeed, the procedure is seemingly designed to discover not how much language pupils have but how little! And even those which seek to measure 'non-verbal' abilities contain implicit demands for language. The front page of an N.F.E.R. Non-verbal Test (Test BD—formerly Non-verbal Test) contains the following instructions:

DO NOT OPEN THIS BOOKLET UNTIL YOU ARE TOLD TO DO SO

FILL IN THE FOLLOWING PARTICULARS:
YOUR FULL NAME   Surname.....................................
                                                      Block Capitals
                           Other Name (s)
NAME OF YOUR SCHOOL
CLASS YOU ARE IN
BOY OR GIRL
YOUR AGE..................YEARS....................MONTHS
DATE OF BIRTH DAY..............MONTH..............YEAR
                  (write the month as a word)
TODAY'S DATE............................19......
READ THE FOLLOWING CAREFULLY:
1. Do not open this booklet until you are told to do so.
2. The test is in sections. You will be told how much time is allowed for each section.
3. When you come to the end of a page, FOLLOW THE INSTRUCTIONS given at the bottom.
4. Each time you are told to stop, STOP WORKING AT ONCE.
5. Work as quickly and as carefully as you can.
6. If when you try a question you find you cannot do it, DO NOT WASTE TIME BUT GO ON TO THE NEXT.
7. Make any alterations in your answers CLEARLY.
8. ASK NO QUESTIONS AT ALL DURING THE TEST.
9. If you should require another pencil, put up your hand.

A certain degree of literacy is here assumed before the pupil can embark upon what is called a 'non-verbal' test, while during the test the pupil will have to make use of language, inside himself, in order to solve the problems posed by the test. The degree of literacy possessed by the pupil at the time of the examination may, or may not, be related to his intellectual capacity. The relationship between capacity to language and intellectual ability is a very complex one, and is not yet sufficiently understood to allow more than tentative assessments to be made in individual cases. Yet the results of such tests, encoded as I.Q., are the basis of labels which categorise pupils throughout their school careers. These labels need contain no explicit reference to I.Q., but their effect is insidious and pervasive, as we see when we consider ways in which pupils are grouped, and regarded, in school.

The basic method of grouping pupils in school is by age, although experiments in grouping children of various ages in teaching groups are being made in some sectors of the educational world. That this procedure is known as 'vertical grouping' emphasises the fact that it is a departure from the norm. The traditional way is to pass children who come into Primary School through the stages of Bottom Infants, Middle Infants, and Top Infants, Bottom Juniors, Middle Juniors and Top Juniors. Likewise, in Secondary Schools pupils proceed from the First to the Fifth Forms, with some going beyond to the Sixth.

When a pupil is judged by his teacher (or teachers) as being unable to keep up with his contemporaries, he will be designated a Slow Learner, and will soon begin to attract one or more of the numerous labels in common use, publicly or privately. This process begins early. There are 'slow tables' in Infant School, and it is not unknown for titles like 'The Problem of the Slow Learner in the Infant School' to be the subject of books, conferences, and papers.

The following extract from 'Notes for Visitors to the School' shows clearly how a Secondary School with, as demonstrated in the first paragraph, a high regard for children as individual, social beings, inevitably sorts them out as pupils, grading them from 'least able' upwards, by means of devices such as 'coarse setting'.

'All forms are non-streamed, the children being allocated on intake from the primary schools in such a way as to secure a spread of academic ability through all first year forms. We make certain exceptions to this random spread: we place children with the same first year form teacher as their brothers and sisters, and we keep together or separate children if advised to do so by the primary school. Since none of the forms is streamed, children can be easily transferred for social reasons, if for example they fail to develop satisfactory relationships with either their peers or their form teacher.

In the first three years, the least able children are withdrawn in small groups for regular tuition in English and/or Mathematics by specialist remedial teachers.

Setting is used to varying degrees in Mathematics, Science and French. In the first year, the six forms are opened out into 8 sets in Mathematics (in each half of the year, one top set, two parallel second sets and a small fourth set), and in Science (one top set, one second set and two parallel third sets). Provision is made for coarse setting late in the year in French, the six forms being timetabled in 2 groups of 3 from which graded sets can be created.'

Into the category of public labels for 'slow learners', that is, labels that are built into the school curriculum, come Less Able, G (for General, as opposed to Academic) and Remedial, or such recent euphemisms as Progress and Opportunity, as in Progress Department and Opportunity Department.

Among private labels, apart from adjectives like 'thick', 'dim' and 'dull', which are in the common language, we find such terms as 'dimbos', 'peasants', 'thugs', 'tail-enders', 'noddies' and 'grots' in frequent use, and the description of particular classes, or groups, as 'the Tip', 'the Sink', 'the Drain', 'a sink-band', or even 'second-band scum'.

There may be an impression that the use of such terms is unknown to the pupils. If so, it is an illusion. You do not need the institutional formality of division by streaming, or setting, or banding, to bring it home to certain categories of pupil that their status within the school is lower than that of certain other categories. There are, as we have already seen, many message systems at work to make the institution's meaning clear to pupils. One very powerful one is the way in which they are referred to by their teachers, in contexts where the categorisation is totally irrelevant.

'He's one of our Remedials. You'd never guess it, would you?' As it happened, no. The boy in question was giving a very promising performance as Puck in a rehearsal of *A Midsummer Night's Dream*.

HEADMASTER (*to visitor*): This is our Remedial Department.
PUPIL (*to teacher, when they had gone*): Sir, what does Remedial mean?

So John Smith, who, outside the school, is a son, a brother, a nephew, a cousin, is, within the school, 'one of our Remedials'. When put into a category which has low status within the school, his chances of ever gaining higher status are slim.

Whether or not his inability, at a particular point in time, to meet the demands of school has been mistaken for an innate incapacity to meet them, the fact remains that he can only be led to a more adequate performance in school by teaching methods which make proper use of what resources he has. This is particularly the case with regard to his language, which lies at the centre of his learning potential. The teacher who described his class, more or less in their hearing, as 'not very bright' was not being over-helpful in giving them an exercise which involved drawing a map and discussing 'The Location of Industry in the British Isles'. In fact, in a very real sense, he was making sure that they couldn't do it, so confirming his judgment and fulfilling his predictions of their ability. A more carefully chosen starting point, within reach of the language and experience of the pupils, might have given them some chance of at least narrowing the gap between what they could bring to the learning situation and what was being demanded of them within it.

# 5 Attitudes to language in school

'I ain't got none, Miss.'
'No, it's not that. It's "I haven't any".'

'There is no reason to believe that any non-standard vernacular is in itself an obstacle to learning. The chief problem is ignorance of language on the part of all concerned.'

*The Logic of Nonstandard English*[10]—W. Labov

A child takes with him into school, a language, and a way of speaking it, that is peculiarly his, his own idiolect, a product, as we saw in chapter 2, of his individual linguistic history. This language is, for the child, the chief means by which he represents his reality to himself; it is also the chief means by which he conducts his relationships with other people; and it constitutes his potential for learning.

He will, in his first school, and thereafter throughout his school career, and indeed throughout life, come into contact with people, teachers and others, who have ideas about language in general and about his in particular. Regrettably, it must be said, many of these ideas still derive from those popular misconceptions of language already referred to as 'folk-linguistic notions of language'. They bear little relationship to any kind of truth about what language is and how it works, but derive from mistaken ideas on such matters as how it is 'proper' or 'correct' to speak.

Since early language learning depends, as we have seen, on the child's ability to grasp intuitively what language is for, and how it works, it is curious that, almost inevitably, the soundly based intuitions about the nature and function language that we display very early in life should become overlaid with culturally

45

transmitted notions about language that are quite at variance with the facts of language.

## Language and speech

The most noticeable feature of a person's language is his way of speaking it, what is sometimes called his accent, or his dialect. Certainly, accent is the most frequent, though not the only, target of the remarks, judgments or criticisms that most people allow themselves to make from time to time about the speech of their fellows.

This person's accent is 'pleasant', or 'musical', or 'country', it has a burr, or a brogue. That person's, on the other hand, is 'ugly', or 'harsh', 'rough' or 'uncouth'. Sometimes the remarks are dressed up as pseudo-linguistic judgments. Speech may be said to be 'slovenly', with 'dropped consonants' or 'dropped aitches', containing 'glottal stops' or 'impure vowels'. It may even be said to have 'no grammar', despite the fact that any language must, by definition, have a grammar. What such remarks really mean is that we don't like a person, or where he comes from, or what he represents, and therefore we don't like his language, and seek to justify the dislike in pseudo-linguistic terms.

It is perhaps significant that the accents which attract the most censure as being 'ugly' or 'uncouth' are those spoken in large conurbations like East London, Birmingham, Liverpool or Tyneside. The fact is that, for a child who grows up with what is regarded as a Birmingham, or Liverpool accent, the accent is not 'harsh', or 'ugly', or 'uncouth'; it is natural. And all those features which his accent is said to have, like 'dropped consonants', 'glottal stops', or whatever it might be, can be shown linguistically to be features of anybody's language. A linguistic perspective gives a very different view of the matter than that enshrined in the folk-linguistic.

We all, as individuals, possess language, and a way of speaking it. In England, there is a form of language known as standard English, and there are various ways of speaking it. That it should be called standard English must not be taken, in any way, to suggest that it is a standard to which all should aspire, or which one does not reach at one's peril. It merely records the fact that it is the form of English most widely and generally spoken, although spoken in different ways, as a journey northwards from Potters Bar will demonstrate. There are also spoken in England

46

various forms of non-standard English, often called dialects, although, as John Pearce points out in *Exploring Language*, chapter 10, not always consistently. The existence of various speech-forms of standard English, and of a number of kinds of non-standard English, constitutes what Abercrombie, in 'RP and Local Accent', the second of his *Studies in Phonetics and Linguistics*,[11] calls 'a rather unfortunate state of affairs—a kind of situation from which many other countries (perhaps all of them) are free.'

The state of affairs is unfortunate largely because of the attitudes towards forms of non-standard English that pervade our society. We have already seen how these attitudes find expression in pseudo-linguistic judgments, and when such attitudes and judgments are directed at pupils in school the effect may be educationally highly damaging.

The short exchange recorded at the head of this chapter took place in the Reception Class of an Infant School, in East London, where the form, 'I ain't got none', is a feature of the local speech. In order to place the exchange in a proper linguistic perspective, it might be useful here to make again, and add to, a number of points about language that were made in Chapter 2.

Language has three levels, phonological, lexico-grammatical and semantic, the level of meaning. 'I ain't got none', like any bit of natural language, operates at all three levels, and operates efficiently. The sounds (which the teacher understood) were organised into a grammatical combination of words, into a combination as grammatical as the alternative offered by the teacher. It is a characteristic of the non-standard forms of English that they contain grammatical constructions which differ from the grammar of standard English. But such constructions are, linguistically, as efficient, and, indeed, as structurally complex, as those found in standard English. They are different, but as bits of language they work equally well. There is no sense in which they are debased. There is no question of the grammar being 'bad' or 'incorrect'. There is moreover no question of the meaning of what the little boy said being in doubt. It was quite unambiguous.

Nevertheless, the teacher thought it right to correct what the child had said. 'No, it's not that.' As far as the child was concerned, it was *that*, and had been for as long as he could, linguistically speaking, remember. 'I ain't got none' was the form that he had grown up with, and had learnt how to use when the occasion

demanded. To say to him, 'It's not that. It's "I haven't any"',
was to say something that, to him, was utterly without meaning.
By what possible criteria could the child interpret the remark, 'It's
not that'? How could he possibly have access to its meaning? If
the teacher wished him to learn the alternative form, and so add
to his linguistic resource in so far as he would then have the possibility of using it when he judged it appropriate (as when, for
example, a teacher thought he ought to use it), then she could
hardly be said to have set up a productive learning situation.
However, it is much more likely that she regarded 'I ain't got
none', as, in some way, the hallmark of a substandard rather than
a non-standard language.

It is sometimes claimed that attitudes towards the accents and
dialects of non-standard English have, in the past ten years or so,
become more tolerant, although one can still be asked such
questions as, 'How can we root out their Birmingham accents'?
It may be that some of the cruder forms of intolerance have been
softened, but disapproval of certain non-standard Englishes is
still widespread. Any attitude towards a pupil's language based
upon such disapproval is bound to have a damaging effect upon
his educational chances.

Devaluing a person's language, which is what you do when you
accuse it of being inferior, is to devalue him. To do this within the
society of the school is to weight the scales against his chances of
success. A barrier has been erected which he has to overcome, even
if it exists only in the teacher's mind, a barrier which is not there
for someone whose language is accepted for what it is. A process of
inevitable failure may then be put in train. Pupils' language is
thought, because of what it sounds like, to be substandard. He
doesn't have much success in school. Therefore others who sound
like him aren't likely to have much success either, because their
teachers come, unconsciously, to think that there are bound to be
limits to what they can achieve. They are thus predisposed to
failure, literally, as soon as they open their mouths.

But the important thing about a pupil's language is not what it
sounds like; it is what he can use it for. It is the meaning potential
that his language gives him, and here again he is likely to run up
against misconceptions about the nature and function of language
that will, in practice, set limits to the enlargement of his range of
meaning potential.

## Functions of language

When describing his seven 'Relevant Models of Language', Halliday remarked of the seventh, the Informative Model, 'This is the only model of language that many adults have.' He meant by this that many adults, including, notably, teachers, seem to think that language is used only for expressing ideas and exchanging information, as indeed it often is in the classroom, despite the range of uses to which they, and those with whom they mix, put language during the course of their daily lives.

Human beings living and working together in the close proximity enforced by an institution like a school have to get on with each other. To do this they need to use language frequently to make what is sometimes called social talk. The starting point of such talk may be the weather, last night's television, gardening, cars, sport, holidays, clothes, domestic problems of various sorts—anything, in fact, about which two or more people can exchange meanings in language for periods ranging from a passing snatch of conversation in the corridor to the lunch-hour. Such talk goes on all the time. But the curious thing is that equivalent talk between pupils is frequently dismissed as 'idle chatter', 'idle gossip' or 'playground talk'. One assumption behind this dismissive judgment seems to be that talk within the school setting that is not inspired, licensed or directed by the teacher is 'idle', and therefore, presumably, profitless. Another assumption seems to be that linguistic exchanges between adults are always, and exclusively, in Halliday's sense, 'informative', that is, concerned with 'processes, persons, objects, abstractions, qualities, states and relations of the real world . . .' A moment's reflection should serve to show how far removed from linguistic reality that is, even at High Table in the Senior Common Room.

It is fatally easy to move from the belief that language used by pupils outside the classroom is of little value, because it does not serve what the teacher regards as an educational purpose, to the belief that they have no worthwhile language at all. This belief is given expression in at least two ways.

'They have no language when they come to me' is a remark that can be heard from teachers at various levels, put in different ways, from Reception Class Teachers in Infant Schools to Lecturers in Colleges and Universities. In fact, it is not very long since a Lecturer in a College of Education was reported as saying, at an Educational Conference in the North of England, 'Many of my

49

own students have to learn their own language at the age of 18 or 19.' A walk through the playground of any Infant School at break or during the lunch-hour, when the place is usually alive with language, is enough to show how far from linguistic truth such an opinion is, whether aimed at five-, eleven- or eighteen-year-olds. Yet, quite recently, a teacher said at a Conference, of pupils who had already been in Secondary School four years, 'They don't even speak English—they just grunt.'

A more subtle, and therefore somewhat more insidious form of this belief about pupils' language is given expression as, 'They have two languages—one that they use in school, and the other that they use outside.' A Junior School Headmaster added, 'I was surprised the other day to find how precise their language is', and thereby revealed what he really thought about 'their' language.

Out of their linguistic resource people have to try to meet the demands of situations in which they find themselves. This entails, among other things, matching the language to the situation, knowing, for example, that talking to the Headmaster requires a different choice of language from that appropriate to a discussion with a peer in the playground. All language users are involved, constantly, in such choices. As a result, all language users may be said to have not two but many languages—even language users of five.

As Eric Ashworth says in *Language in the Junior School*,

'By the time that the children arrive in the Primary School, they will all have learned to perform their language with a high degree of skill. Even the most backward child there will know how to operate complex systems of words and how to select from among grammatical systems in order to make a range of meanings that is enormously wide. So great will be the ability of the children that it would not be stretching the imagination to call them experts.'

It is these 'experts' who are then said, in school, to 'have no language'. As it was put in an Infant School scheme of work, 'Where language is entirely lacking a cautious approach brings best results.' Pupils are then written off as 'inarticulate', or 'unable to express themselves', or 'unable to communicate'.

We live our lives in a succession of contexts which are socially constructed (and this includes the context of the classroom) and which appear to us as situations in which we can mean something, or we can't. We can mean something when the language used puts meaning within our reach, and when our role in the situation makes it possible for us to contribute meaning.

The function of education is to increase, for the pupil, the possibility of making meaning. This can be done only by enabling him to draw upon his linguistic resource, which in turn can happen only if the teacher accepts that resource for what it is, and assists the pupil to exploit and expand it.

When the pupil's language is disvalued because of what it sounds like, or its potential underestimated because of misconceptions about the way in which language functions, then indeed 'educational endeavour' can become very difficult.

# 6  Demands on pupils' language

'First formers do ask such stupid questions.'

A pupil in school is constantly faced with demands upon his linguistic resource. In one sense, he is, in this respect, in no different situation from most other human beings most of the time. As human beings we live by and through language. But pupils not only live by language, they learn through language—simultaneously. And the business of learning entails responding to demands for language related, in highly specialised ways, to specific contexts which are sometimes quite remote from the kind of context in which the language of every day functions.

We have already seen that the way in which we are regarded as human beings within the community of the institution will have its effect on our ability to use language successfully within the institution. By this is meant, in the terms in which language is conceived in this book, the ability of the individual pupil to draw upon his linguistic resource in order to meet the demands for making meanings in language. And before he can begin to meet the demands, he must, of course, be able to understand them, that is, he must be able to reach the meaning carried by the language used to formulate the demand.

In this chapter, we shall look closely at the nature of typical demands made upon the language of pupils in school, and in the next we shall ask what opportunities are provided for pupils to develop the abilities to meet these demands.

Such an examination could be made, in principle, at any stage of the educational career. The predicament is fundamentally the same, whether we are considering first entry to school at 5, transfer to Junior School at 7, to Middle School at 8 or 9, Secondary School

52

at 11 or 13, Sixth Form College or College of Further Education at 16 plus, or any of the institutions of Higher Education thereafter. Demands will always be made upon a pupil's capacity to put meaning into language, and judgments will constantly be made, on criteria operated by the teacher, upon his apparent ability to meet those demands adequately and, usually, quickly. The point of reference for the analysis in this chapter will, however, be transfer to Secondary School at 11.

There are a number of reasons for choosing this point. Eric Ashworth, in *Language in the Junior School*, in this series, has taken a critical look at the language experience that pupils can expect to have in school between 5 and 11. Despite the development, in some areas, of Middle Schools, it remains true that most pupils in England transfer to some form of secondary education at 11, and it is also true that this transfer brings with it inevitable difficulties for the pupil, not least in the area of language.

Any transfer from one school to another involves the pupil in the task of finding his way through what we have called the 'hidden curriculum' of the new institution, but transfer to some form of secondary education brings with it particular difficulties which derive from the fact that secondary education is still, to a large extent, subject-oriented. This means, in effect, that he will be taught by teachers for whom the language of a particular subject, or subject area (like Humanities, or Social Studies, or Creative Arts) has, through long experience and use, become very familiar.

It is very easy for a subject specialist, immersed in it as he is, to believe that the language of his own subject is part of what he imagines to be a 'common language', the kind of language that everyone has, or should have, in common. Such an assumption is, of course, yet another of the misconceptions about language use discussed in the last chapter. It is at one with the demand for 'good plain English' that is so frequently heard.

'Why can't he put it in good plain English?'

'It' may be anything, or rather any *meaning*, according to who 'he' is, where 'he' is, and the meaning that he is trying to language. The assumption clearly is that there is an available language into which any meaning can be encoded, irrespective of what that meaning is, or of the audience for whom it is intended, and of how much meaning and language they already share with the speaker (or writer). OUR MIRAGE SHOULD FOIL IRISH GAMBLE is 'good plain English' to those who have access to its meaning.

To those who don't, it may seem like gibberish. But, given the context, with all that that implies about the nature of his audience and the knowledge he shares with them, the writer of the headline was being plainly meaningful. Language use must always take account of the audience for whom it is intended, and the situation in which it is being used.

A first-former in a Secondary School will arrive, on a typical school day, at the appointed time, join up with some of his peers, and make his way to the place within the school where, for him, Registration takes place. He will probably take part in some form of Assembly, at the end of which it will not be unknown for him to have to listen to a succession of notices taking twenty minutes to read out. Thereafter, he (or she) will move about the school as a member of a group, or as a member of different groups brought together for different purposes, according to the organisation of the school. As he does so, he will be responding to language with language, meaning with meaning, or trying to. It may be the language of his friends, outside the class-room situation or the language of the teacher inside the class-room situation; in the main, language as speech. If he is particularly unlucky, his efforts to participate in the sharing of meaning will be rewarded with the kind of remark quoted at the head of the chapter.

## Spoken and written

In the classroom situation there will come, sooner or later, demands for language as writing. There is speech, and there is writing. Being literate is having the ability to move from spoken to written language, and back again, freely and at will. In the linguistic history of each individual, just as in the history of the evolution of human language, speech comes before writing. Learning to be literate requires the pupil, at some stage, to invest in mastering the writing system that knowledge of language, and how it works, that he acquired in its spoken form by living and growing up with it.

The relationship of written language to the spoken language to which it corresponds is a complex one, more complex than is often acknowledged, and than is apparently assumed in, for example, phonic approaches to the teaching of reading, or traditional attitudes to spelling. Spoken language consists of sounds made with the mouth, written language of marks made with the hand. Spoken language occurs normally in face-to-face situations in which language and other channels can be used together to convey the meaning which it is intended to convey. Moreover, as we speak in such a situation, we can register the effect of what we are meaning on other people present, and can modify what we say as we go along.

Written language exists not in time but in space. It lacks the immediacy of context provided by the face-to-face situation, and cannot make use of such characteristics of speech as intonation, pausing and stress. At the same time it has features, like punctuation marks and capital letters, that have no equivalent in speech. It is usually required in longer, perhaps more complex, structures than spoken language, which consists typically of what have been described as 'structured chunks of syntax and meaning' rather than complete sentences. This tends to require more sophisticated demands on the resources of language itself. It normally requires a more formal style, in the sense in which Martin Joos used the term in his book, *The Five Clocks*,[12] than is the case with spoken language. It, also, as far as school is concerned, tends to be 'informational' type language.

Written language, moreover, is normally a written form of the standard language. Written forms of non-standard languages, or dialects, are usually confined to characters in novels or pieces in local papers by writers trying to preserve local dialects. Such forms are not functional, in the sense that they are not forms of language in everyday use in the life of the community.

The speaker of non-standard language has, if he is to meet the demands made upon him in school (demands which are also non-functional, although in a different way, in that they are not related to life outside the school), to acquire an ability to handle the written form of the standard language in general use in the community. This is not a necessarily more difficult task than that facing the speaker of a form of standard English, as Labov insists in *The Logic of Non-standard English*,[8] although the task will be made more difficult, in practice, for the child whose teacher has a less than proper regard for his language, and fails to set up learning situations which will allow him to invest in his new task that knowledge of language which he already has.

It is vital that a pupil adds to his linguistic resource the ability to operate in the written medium, because the most important demands in the educational context will be for written language,

55

important if for no other reason than that all the significant judgments about his ability and progress will be based upon his performance in the written medium.

Failure to acquire the ability to operate freely in the written medium, failure that is to become literate, brings with it disadvantages that accumulate with the passage of time, since the further one proceeds in the school system the more pressing become the demands for written work, and the slimmer the chances of achieving literacy if you haven't already done so. Despite a great deal of dedicated work going on in Remedial departments, there has so far been little serious attempt to evolve teaching techniques based upon sound linguistic principles.

## Classroom language

The first-former we left on a previous page will move from lesson to lesson, from English, say, to French, to Science, to Music, to Woodwork. . . . In each subject he will be faced with language demands. These will take the form, initially, of a need to understand, and perhaps respond in the form of a question to, the teacher who is setting up the lesson; of having, perhaps, to read instructions, or some form of text; and/or of having to do some writing. It is an illuminating experience to spend a day with a first form in a Secondary School, taking note of the language demands made upon them.

These are extracts from books in use in the first forms of a Secondary School in the subjects mentioned in the last paragraph:

I. ENGLISH

Chapter 1 The Hall by the Tarn

Two figures stood in the darkness, a man and a boy. Behind them the pine woods sighed, as though overcome by a great and unnameable sadness, the melancholy sound made by all ancient forests. As the round moon came from behind a bank of cloud, throwing its silver light over the rough and rocky land below, the two figures peered down into the valley beneath them, their heavy cloaks sweeping away from them in the night-wind that blew towards them from the woods. A great white seabird circled above their heads, crying harshly and pitifully in the moonlight. They shuddered at the sound, looking up in dread. The man's bearded lips moved silently, as though he spoke a charm against the witches of the night. The moon slowly withdrew behind the

56

straggling cloudbank, and for a moment there was utter darkness once more.

Then suddenly, from the valley, came a surge of flame, a great red and orange spurting-up of light. A thick cloud of oily smoke rose above it, into the night air. A flock of birds flew, twittering up from the valley, to the woods. The two watchers drew in their breath as the many wings beat above them in the darkness.

Now the fire-glow spread and its angry light flared out over a black tarn nearby, so that the man and boy saw reflected in the sombre water every shape and hue of the flames.

*The Wizard of Earthsea*—Ursula Le Guin

## 2. FRENCH

### A. MON ALBUM FRANAÇIS

Start to keep a French scrapbook. Label the cover 'Mon album français' and decorate it in a suitable way, with pictures of France, French stamps, labels or postcards. The scrapbook will be used to collect interesting items and information about France and French-speaking countries. Suggestions will be made for the use of the scrapbook, but you should also try to think of ideas of your own.

Start to keep a list of new items in your scrapbook.

Under suitable headings (e.g. Dans la salle de classe; A la maison) draw pictures of objects whose French names you know, and label them in French. As an alternative to drawing, stick in pictures which you have cut out from magazines.

### B. Divide into two teams, 'les Français' and 'les Anglais'.

Ask your opposite number questions such as:

Oú est le professeur?

Qu'est-ce que c'est?

Est-ce que c'est un stylo?

Use only the names of objects which you have already met. Points are gained both for correct questions and correct answers.

*Audio-Visual French* (Longman)

## 3. SCIENCE

11  Here are four lists of things:

    a  Brass, glass, grass.

    b  Daisy, rose, flint, mushroom, wheat, seaweed.

    c  Seawood, woodlouse, daffodil, snake, salt, mouse, bracken, crab, whale.

    d  Slate, chalk, water, air, aluminium, iron, oil, lead, mercury, asbestos, tadpole, rubber, brick.

Choose one item in each list which you think is the 'odd man out'.
Why do you think so?
Your friends disagree with you, and each other, about all four lists.
Imagine choices for your friends and their reasons.
Is there any reason why one thing in each list must be the right choice?
Do their reasons make you change your mind? Do your reasons change theirs?

*Nuffield Combined Science*, Book 1

4. MUSIC

## 11 THE KNIGHTS OF THURINGIA

### The Story

Most people have heard of the troubadours and trouvères, nobly-born poets and song-writers who lived in France during the twelfth and thirteenth centuries. Sometimes they sang their own works in courtly circles; sometimes they paid professional minstrels to do so. King Richard the Lion-Heart was a troubadour, and Blondel was his faithful minstrel.

About the time of the troubadours the German-speaking countries had their Minnesingers, chief of whom were the knights Walter von der Vogelweide, Wolfram von Eschenbach, and Tannhäuser. Like the troubadours, they had a strict code of rules governing their art and their personal conduct, and they met periodically to hold friendly tournaments of song in the castle of the Wartburg in Thuringia.

The Wartburg is one of the most romantic places in Europe. In later years it became the refuge of Martin Luther, where he translated the New Testament into German. Long before that time, however, and even before the coming of the Minnesingers, it was believed that the goddess Holda, whose worship gradually became confused with that of the Roman goddess Venus, reigned beneath a neighbouring mountain.

*Legends in Music*—John Horton

5. WOODWORK

3  Plans and Elevations

The main purpose of making drawings is to give us a small picture on a flat (or two-dimensional) drawing paper, which we can easily carry about, of a large solid (or three-dimensional) object.

To see how this is done let us investigate how a solid rectangular prism resting on a flat level plane is represented in a two-dimensional diagram.

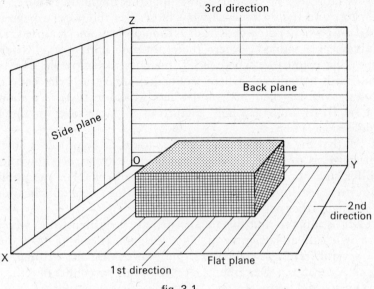

3rd direction

Z

Back plane

Side plane

O

Y

2nd direction

X

Flat plane

1st direction

fig. 3.1

Fig. 3.1 shows the prism resting on the flat plane

*Technical Drawing*

A fairly rapid glance will reveal that very different kinds of meaning are involved.

'Behind them, the pine woods sighed, as though overcome by a great and unnameable sadness, the melancholy sound made by all ancient forests.'

'The scrapbook will be used to collect interesting items and information about France and French-speaking countries.'

'd   Slate, chalk, water, air, aluminium, iron, oil, lead, mercury, asbestos, tadpole, rubber, brick.

Choose one item in each list which you think is the 'odd man out'.

'Like the troubadours they had a strict code of rules governing their art and their personal conduct, and they met periodically to hold friendly tournaments of song in the castle of the Wartburg in Thuringia.'

'The main purpose of making drawings is to give us a small picture on a flat (or two-dimensional) drawing paper, which we can easily carry about, of a large solid (or three-dimensional) object.'

As he reads, the reader draws upon his linguistic resource to try to reach the meaning of what he sees on the page, a page in this case, where pine woods 'sigh as though overcome by a great and unnameable sadness', where there are such entities as 'French-speaking countries', where 'lead, mercury, asbestos' lie side by side with a 'tadpole', where troubadours have a 'strict code of rules governing their art', and where we can easily carry about 'a small "two-dimensional" picture of a "large solid (or three-dimensional) object".'

All that the reader of this book has to do, as he proceeds down the page, is to reach the meanings of the extracts, see how they differ, and appreciate the point in the argument. For the pupil, however, reaching the meaning is merely the entry qualification to some further activity.

Let us suppose that this further activity is written work, which we will call an assignment. This assignment might take one of several forms. It could be a piece of continuous writing, an essay, perhaps, 'Describe......', 'Give an account of ......', 'Why are/did/were ......?', 'What were the reasons for ......', or some 'creative writing'. It might be in the form of notes, in 'English', on troubadours, for example, or in the form of answers to questions, such as those posed in extract 3 ('Why do you think so?') or as a so-called Comprehension Test to extract 1.

The pupil now has to draw upon his resource to language meaning in the written medium, and in a form of the written medium which has its own conventions. What these conventions are, as they apply to style, setting out, etc, must, if he is to take account of them, form part of his resource as knowledge about language, and how it is to be used in a particular context.

A Comprehension Test based upon passage 1 might be presented to the pupil like this:

1. Why does the author say that the pine woods 'sighed'?
2. What does 'melancholy' mean?
3. What other word could the author have used for 'peered'?
4. Why do you think they looked up at the bird 'in dread'?
5. What does 'as though he spoke a charm against the witches of the night' mean?
6. Why does the author call the cloudbank 'straggling'?
7. Put into your own words 'reflected in the sombre water every shape and hue of the flames'.
8. Give two examples of metaphors used in the passage.

Are answers to questions 1 and 2 to be given as 'one-word'

answers? Or are they required in the form of sentences? The pupil must possess knowledge such as this before he can begin to deal with the 'Comprehension Test' itself, that is to say, to play about with the bits and pieces of language of which the Test consists. What in fact his attempts to answer the questions will reveal of his understanding of the passage in question is doubtful. And what this kind of dabbling in language in such a narrow context subject to such rigid constraints can be expected to reveal of any general capacity is even more doubtful.

The questions on the 'four lists of things' in the extract from the Science book were put in a form which was the result of a deliberate attempt to make the style more informal, to shift it nearer to 'everyday language'. This obviously begs certain questions about the relationship of spoken to written language, and about the relationship of the functional language of every day to the language of scientific questions. Nevertheless, it does represent an attempt to shift the language of the assignment nearer to the language of the pupil, although trying to 'Imagine choices for your friends and their reasons' is quite a formidable task.

Pupils, then, are expected to know the rules of so many games: to know what an 'essay' or 'composition' is; to know what features of writing make it, in the eyes of the teacher, especially 'creative'; how to set down answers in tests; how to make notes, whether for private, revisionary purposes or for being marked as an accurate record of what has been reducd to note form. All such knowledge *about* language must form part of linguistic resource if, out of that resource, demands are to be adequately met. And if they are to become part of linguistic resource, then opportunity must be given for this to happen. Opportunity and time.

Early language learning takes place with almost unbelievable speed. Later language learning, or, rather, extension of linguistic resource, takes time, time to allow new possibilities of making meanings, and languaging them, to be added to the potential that one already possesses. This may be particularly the case if the meaning, and the language which is to carry it, is remote from one's experience. And time is, so it seems, always at a premium in school, where syllabuses have to be got through, or examinations prepared for. 'You should have finished by now.' But for those who haven't finished there is rarely going to be another opportunity, because the next lesson may bring something new, some fresh demands on capacity for meaning. Once again, it is those furthest away from making contact with the desired meaning

61

who suffer, and whose performance in the classroom is written off.

It is true, of course, that pupils do not spend all their time in classrooms with specialist teachers who make highly specialised demands on their language. Of the time spent in school, from nine to four, five days a week, for some forty weeks a year, some is spent in breaks, lunch-hours, and in what are sometimes called 'out-of-school activities', mixing with and relating to peers and teachers. Nevertheless, position within the school, as a pupil, is essentially based upon performance in the classroom, and, within that context, upon ability to handle written language. Most school reports consist of comments made by subject teachers, with space allocated at the bottom for the comments of form-masters, house-masters, or others responsible for the 'pastoral' side. Many Parents' Evenings consist of meetings with, and reports from, subject teachers.

All this adds up to the fact that public judgments on a pupil's achievement within the school may be made upon a comparatively limited part of his endeavour, that part, perhaps, in which he finds most difficulty in performing adequately. The effect must be to make the rest, in comparison, seem irrelevant.

# 7 How are pupils expected to learn how to mean?

'I've found a very squashed map of Great Britain.'
'It's like a tree with a bird on it and the bird flying down off it.'
'Mine's shaped like an oak leaf.'
'A bit like . . . very small ice flakes. . . .'

These snippets of language were recorded during a lesson in which some 11-year-old girls were looking into a microscope and trying to describe what they could see. What they were looking at were slides made by rubbing a finger inside the cheek, and then drawing the finger across a glass slide. They were, in fact, looking at, and trying to describe, what the biologist would call cells.

The lesson was of a kind that has become familiar in Nuffield Science, whereby the pupils must discover for themselves, with the teacher acting as a guide rather than an instructor. The pupils in the lesson in question tried hard, and sometimes colourfully, but without success, to find a language that their teacher would accept.

Their predicament was like that of anybody faced with a specific demand to make new meanings out of his language. You bring to the situation your linguistic resource, and endeavour to draw upon it, as best you can within the constraints of the situation, for a response that you hope will prove adequate.

These pupils discovered that their response was not adequate because their teacher would not accept their attempts to describe what they saw. '. . . a very squashed map of Great Britain' is not the language into which you put meaning in Biology. Nor is, 'It's like a tree with a bird on it and the bird flying down off it.' Creative writing, perhaps. Biology, no.

The important question for these pupils is, then, what chance are they going to be given to acquire the ability to use language— that is, to make meaning—in biology lessons in a way that will satisfy their teacher? Put like this, it is, of course, seen to be the important question for all pupils faced with unfamiliar demands upon their linguistic resource.

We will assume, for the time being, that movement towards increased ability to make new meanings will typically start with spoken language, probably with the teacher talking and the pupil trying to reach the meaning of what the teacher is putting into language. This may not be easy, especially if the teacher is introducing an area of meaning that is wholly unfamiliar.

What, in effect, the pupil is being asked to do is to take in what the teacher is saying, and try to match it to what he already knows, to see if he can reach its meaning. The operation may take time, more time than is allowed, because there is a lesson plan to be carried through in forty minutes.

Some recent work, including particularly that of Douglas Barnes,[13] has focused on the nature of linguistic interaction in the classroom, interaction, that is, between teacher and pupil. The investigations have thrown some light on the opportunities given to pupils, in typical classroom situations, to talk their way, as Barnes puts it, 'into understanding' or 'into new meanings'. The findings are not very hopeful.

Many so-called discussion lessons consist of talk by the teacher (it is said that the average lesson begins with fifteen minutes uninterrupted talk by the teacher) followed by a teacher-dominated pattern of interaction. Questions are asked, and elicit short, perhaps one-word, answers. Pupils pursuing their own attempts to make meanings often get little encouragement. Their answers may not be accepted because they don't happen to be the 'right one', or they may apparently be accepted but re-phrased by the teacher in his language. In fact, what often happens (and pupils themselves have pointed this out) is that a kind of guessing game ensues, with the pupil trying to guess what is in the teacher's mind. As always, those who guess quickest find the most favour.

Moreover, the fact that one pupil has guessed the right answer, and has thereby shown that he has reached at least part of the teacher's meaning, may be taken as evidence that others (perhaps most of the class) are similarly within reach. This, of course, may be a complete misconception. Many may be in the situation described by the second-former who confided, in a moment of candour, to the mature student on teaching practice who was taking them for English, 'Most of us don't know what the bloody hell you're talking about.'

64

Such a misconception will have the effect of excluding, perhaps permanently, those who are wrongly assumed to have reached a certain stage of participation in meaning. This exclusion may be reinforced by the teacher who has little sympathy for those who take time to understand, the kind of teacher of whom it was once said, 'You were all right if you knew what she was talking about. She had no time for you if you didn't.' Such an attitude not only places responsibility for reaching meaning where it is least able to be assumed, on the pupil. It operates, inevitably, to the disadvantage of those who are farthest away from the meanings which it is desired they should gain access to.

The process of gaining understanding will at some stage be accompanied by demands for written language, of various sorts. Some have already been mentioned, like essays, compositions, descriptions, notes and tests. The list could be extended to include the writing up of scientific experiments, the drawing of diagrams in which language and diagram operate together to make meaning, the doing of various kinds of exercise. (*Language in Use*,[14] especially the units in Themes A and G, gives examples of a large number of highly context-specific uses of language.)

If the process is as we have described it, then what productive opportunities can the pupil expect to be given to extend his resource to meet such demands for written language as are made of him?

Can he, for example, expect to be given opportunities to rehearse what he wants to mean, either in speech or writing, to make mistakes, to try again, before he, at length, hopefully, comes to a reasonably adequate attempt? Or will he be expected to discharge his assignment in a once-for-all attempt, something that not even the most experienced writer, faced with an unfamiliar (or even a familiar!) demand, would expect to make do with?

Can he expect that, when he has produced an attempt to meet the teacher's demands, it will be the subject of informed comment and encouragement? Or can he expect that it will receive what Angus McIntosh, in *Language and Style*,[15] referred to as 'little more than a series of red lights or warnings' about particular points of usage?

Too often, the criteria on which these 'warnings' are based are misconceived or inappropriate or inconsistent, and their effect is to mislead or to confuse. Attention may be drawn to grammatical 'solecisms' like 'split infinitives' or reduced forms such as 'haven't' or 'aren't', which in the context of an attempt to make meaning may be comparatively trivial considerations. Comments like 'Never use slang' may be written in the margin of an essay where, indeed, certain kinds of slang expressions may be inappropriate, as though slang were a kind of linguistic offence which no self-respecting language user ever resorted to. The pupil, if he knows what slang is, knows also that this is not true, because he hears it used, as it is in appropriate contexts, every day, including by his teachers.

Moreover, the criteria applied to the marking of 'creative writing' in English, to essays in English, to writing in other subjects, where, for example, the regard paid to such features of the writing system as spelling and punctuation may differ widely, are liable to drastic variation. The pupil, who may be given little opportunity to discover what criteria are likely to apply, is left in a state of confusion.

He may also be given little opportunity to acquire the ability to satisfy the criteria which are applied, since the language activities that he is asked to engage in, supposedly to help him remedy his defects, suffer the crippling disadvantages of resting upon the same kind of linguistically inadequate foundations that underlie approaches to many other aspects of the learning situation in which he is placed.

'Use the following words in sentences to show clearly that you understand their meaning: antediluvian, belligerent, cynosure, discernment, ephemeral, garrulous, hierarchy, idiosyncrasy, jeopardy, mnemonic, obsequies, panegyric.'

An exercise typical of those set in preparation for certain kinds of examination in English.

Fill in the gaps in the columns.

| Masculine | Feminine |
| --- | --- |
| Prince | Princess |
| Nephew | — |
| — | Spinster |
| Duke | — |
| — | Mistress |
| Manservant | — |
| — | Vixen |
| Monk | — |
| — | Bride |
| Cock | — |

An exercise typical of those which appear in course-books intended for use in English lessons.

66

'After her toilet Molly was —— and ——.

Which of the following words fits into the gaps? (a) frisky; (b) lazy; (c) contented; (d) grumpy.'

An exercise typical of 'comprehension exercises' to be found in books in use in Primary Schools. (It should be added, perhaps, that Molly is a cat!)

If the object of his going to school is to enable the pupil to increase his ability to make meanings in language, what value have exercises like these—and others of similar kinds? They are unrelated to anything of an on-going nature that he might be doing, and they yield no insights into the nature and function of language that can subsequently be invested in the task of making new meanings. The bits of language, usually at a lexical (not even the lexico-grammatical) level, that pupils are asked to play about with are randomly chosen. In the example above, spinster, duchess, mistress, maidservant, vixen, nun, bride and hen, all admittedly in a category 'feminine', appear together. In what context other than an exercise in an English course-book would they so appear?

Activities such as these derive from no theory of language and learning which might lead us to suppose that, by engaging in them, pupils would be likely to increase their ability to perform adequately in tasks calling for other uses of written language, especially extended, connected use of written language. Far more about the nature and function of language must be taken into account if activities are to be designed that will enable pupils to invest in them productively the linguistic resource that they have, so that they might emerge from them with their meaning potential enlarged.

The depth of knowledge about language ideally required by those, teachers and others, who make pupils engage in language activities which purport to help pupils extend their range of ability to handle language is well illustrated by Ruqaiya Hasan in the paper she wrote for the first series of Papers in Linguistics and English Teaching, called *Grammatical cohesion in spoken and written English*.[16] Its subject matter can be most easily illustrated by comparing the following two passages:

'The other day, at my local supermarket, I was in the queue behind the mother of a young boy. Thick yarn and eye-catching patterning give these country classics a new look. When working out plans for a new garden or replanning an old one, you must think of the years ahead. It has been said, with a little bit of humour, and a tiny chance of truth, that Health is good for you.'

'In the last resort we cannot evaluate any specimen of language —and deciding whether or not it forms a text is a prerequisite to any further evaluation of it—without knowing something about its subject-matter and its function. We need to know what in linguistics is called its "context of situation", and there are three aspects to the context of situation of a text: its relation to human experience (the 'subject-matter' in the widest sense), its setting (by whom it is addressed, to whom, and in what type of social interaction), and its purpose and scope within that setting.'

(The word 'text' had earlier in the paper been defined as 'any piece of language, spoken or written, of whatever length, that does form an integrated whole.')

The first is a random selection of sentences, assembled by taking the first sentence from each of four features in a magazine. The second is an extract from Hasan's paper itself, a paper which describes the linguistic devices which are used to bind language together, those devices which enable us to tell at a glance that the second passage forms a piece of integrated language, while the first is a mere agglomeration of sentences.

The quotation from Hasan's paper was chosen deliberately to illustrate the factors which the author thought it important to bring into reckoning when introducing her subject. It is significant that when she stresses the importance of taking subject matter and function into account, she regards this as, 'in its widest sense', considering its 'relation to human experience', and that when she proposes to look at its setting, she takes this to include 'what type of social interaction' is involved in the writing. Far from regarding a piece of text as something that is produced, and can be looked at, in isolation, she insists that it must be looked at from a functional viewpoint, as a piece of language produced for a purpose, at a particular time, in a particular place.

Texts produced by pupils in school, in English lessons, in History lessons, in Science lessons, in examinations, or whatever, are in this respect no different from texts produced in other places by other people. They, too, relate ultimately to 'human experience', to that tradition of human experience which has shaped the demand for a certain kind of text, and to the 'human experience' of the pupil asked for the text. The pupil, no less than other producers of texts, is subject to the constraints of the 'social interaction' at the point of production of the text, that between himself and his teacher in the class-room.

If, then, we are to consider the situation of the pupil in the

68

class-room who has been given the task of writing something, with a view to commenting on the adequacy of what he produces, we must consider what chance he has of relating what he has been asked to do to what he already knows. What can he draw upon, in terms of his ability to language meaning, that is relevant to the task in hand? Tasks which are within his range will give him a chance of adequate performance, and the kind of reinforcement that adequate performance brings. Tasks beyond his range will bring inadequate performance, brought home to him, often publicly, by all or some of the usual apparatus of marking, marks, grades, positions in form, examinations, and reports, which, all too often, may have the effect of humiliating, rather than encouraging.

This chapter has put the question, 'How are pupils expected to learn how to mean?' The best way of learning how to mean is by trying, perhaps by only partly succeeding, and trying again until one does succeed.

There are signs that, in some schools, pupils are being given the opportunity to acquire experience in situations. Unfortunately, however, when attempts are made to set up situations in which pupils can gain experience of learning how to mean, some are rendered less than helpful by the ideas about language that inform them, as in the case of the following notes drawn up for the guidance of teachers conducting Mock Interviews for school-leavers in a Secondary School.

### MOCK INTERVIEW

TEACHER  Good afternoon, Miss Green. Please sit down.

PUPIL  Thank you. (5 points.)

T  Your name has been sent to me by the Youth Employment Service for a position as a Junior Shorthand Typist. Is that correct?

P  (Yes, Mr. Brown told me to call—5 pts.) (Yes only—2 pts.)

T  Very well. What school did you attend?

P  (Wensum Road Secondary School—5 pts. No pts for any other answer.)

T  So you know Mr. Black, then?

P  (Yes, he is my Headmaster—5 pts.) (Yes only—2 pts.)

T  Indeed, Mr Black has sent me some very good girls in the past. I hope if we appoint you, you will be equally as good.

P  (I hope so—No pts.) (I will do my best—5 pts.)

| | |
|---|---|
| T | What were your best subjects at school? |
| P | (Maths, English, Shorthand, Typewriting—5 pts.) (Other subjects—No pts.) |
| T | What are your hobbies? |
| P | (Reading, dancing, stamp collecting, etc.—5 pts.) (No pts for listening to Pop records, etc.) |
| T | Do you like reading? |
| P | (Yes—3 pts.) (Yes, very much—5 pts.) |
| T | When did you last read a book? |
| P | (Last week—5 pts.) |
| T | What was it called? |
| P | (5 pts for a classic, 3 pts for a schoolgirl's book, no pts for anything else.) |
| T | Well, that is enough about your hobbies. Do you know what we make here? |
| P | (5 for a yes, 3 for a no.) |
| T | We make electrical equipment. Do you think you will like working here? |
| P | (Yes, very much—5 pts.) (Yes—3 pts.) |
| T | Have you any questions to ask me? |
| P | (5 pts for each question about salaries, holidays, etc.) |

# 8 What is to be done?

*Guidance on Marking of Written Work*
These notes have been prepared at the Headmaster's request
(see Staff Bulletin No. 2, 11th September 1968) as a *supplement*
to the section 'Correction of Written Work' of the syllabus
(pp 5–6).

Extract from English Syllabus

There follows a list of aims such as can be found in many English
syllabuses. Such lists are likely to include some or all of the
following:

To draw the pupils' attention to the merits and the shortcomings in the content and mode of expression of their work.

To rectify specific errors in spelling, punctuation, grammar
and usage.

To promote understanding of sentence structure, para-
graphing, punctuation, parts of speech, and grammar, as
required for the improvement of style and the correction of
error, accuracy in spelling and the efficient use of a dictionary.

To avoid mistakes of punctuation, grammar, spelling and
idiom.

To encourage syntactical correctness.

To correct major errors, e.g. misrelated participles, gerunds,
infinitives or elliptical clauses; faulty sentence structure, e.g.
serious lack of unity—Eskimoes are good hunters and they are
few in number, etc.

To keep a remorseless watch for slovenly or lazy English.

The essential weakness of statements of aims like this is that
they wobble from one level to another, without ever beginning
to suggest an existence at the most important level of all, the level
of meaning. There is no explicit recognition that what a writer is

trying to do is to put elements and structures together to make meaning; no attempt to define priorities in spotting where there might be weakness. There are no strategies recommended which might be used to encourage a pupil to build on what he can do in order to achieve a more adequate level of performance. 'Shortcomings' must be pointed out, errors 'rectified', 'mistakes' avoided. It is a purely penal approach, on a par with the custom of setting essays as impositions.

How could aims such as these be translated into any kind of action that would help the writer of the following?

*describe som of the advontages of owning your own bugness and some of the problems you are liney to be faced with otworking a new busoness*

*The advontages having your owne place of your owne is yoou ore in chaving of the place your Slove you tell ~~vuin~~ ~~petu~~ your staff wont to do. If I had a solon of my oune I ~~wood~~ wold have a small one but I thike it is too much ~~Res fotte~~ independepndance off yowur slove. problems you wloud have to faced, is how ~~peste~~ ~~ut~~ people be in your shop and be nice to them if you dont be nice to ~~him~~ them you will loze them ond ~~lose~~ your busseinesos. If you are howing a place of your windows should be desperdy nicely, befoure I ~~setur~~ A business I woild love to have lote off money and pople to hlep me start my business. The best way would to Avertis in the paper for hlep for hairthies And when I hove hlep I will pople see the gooma if thay good*

The writer is a 16-year-old girl, following a course in Hairdressing at a College of Further Education. She has been asked, according to the title of her piece, to, 'Describe some of the advantages of owning your own business and some of the problems you are likely to be faced with in starting a new business'. She is not fully literate, in the sense in which it was defined on page 54. Her linguistic resource does not include the facility of moving easily from spoken to written language. She is not, on the other hand, wholly illiterate. The meaning of what she has written is accessible, on the whole fairly readily, to anyone who is both literate and sympathetic. How, then, can she be helped to greater literacy, helped to extend her linguistic resource to include the possibility of encoding meaning more successfully in written language?

Perhaps the first point to make is to suggest that any assignment she is given should be more realistic, in at least two ways. It should be more nearly within her reach, so that she will have a chance of performing adequately, with all that that implies about the effects of success. In the second place, assignments should be more closely related to the purpose for which language is actually used. People may think about, and discuss with others, 'the advantages of owning your own business.' If it is remotely possible that they may, indeed, one day own their own business, they will be wise to seek advice on 'some of the problems you are likely to be faced with in starting a new business'. Such advice will be needed not only from those who have already set themselves up in business but from bank managers, estate agents, manufacturers' representatives, and so on. You will certainly have to have interviews, ranging from informal chats to formal requests. You will almost certainly have to write letters asking for advice, appointments, and quotations, and you may have to use language for other functions in the course of setting up your business. But whatever else you do in the course of setting yourself up in business you are unlikely to have to write an essay on the subject—unless you did a course in a department in a College where someone thought it a useful assignment to give you.

Given that the writer of the piece was asked to describe (only) 'some of the advantages . . .' and (only) 'some of the problems . . .'; that this requires a knowledge, and an ability to make meaning, that in her case she quite certainly will not have; that she does not handle the writing system easily, whereas the assignment demands a fairly sophisticated ability—given all this, what kind of attempt did she make? The answer must surely be, 'Not bad at all.'

She begins by wanting to mean something like, 'The advantage of having a place of your own is that you are in charge of the place yourself. You tell your staff what to do.' That is, perhaps, how it would be represented in the writing system, with traditional orthography and conventional punctuation.

The girl herself wrote down two ways of languaging her first bit of meaning: having your own place and having a place of your own. It is a characteristic feature of spoken language that bits of two (or even more) structures come out entwined together. What seems to happen is that, at some point in the languaging-of-meaning process where we are planning how to say what we want to mean, more than one option presents itself. We choose one, but occasionally bits of discarded choices remain embedded in what we actually say.

The same thing can happen when we are writing our meaning; bits of two constructions can appear on the page under our pen. Usually, because we can see what we have done, we realise what has happened and cross out the intruding bits, if not at once then on re-reading. This girl had not done so. The chances are that if she had been asked to-read, given the time to re-read, or asked to read aloud, what she had written she, too, would have realised what she had done.

There are, of course, other ways in which what she wrote differs from what would be generally regarded as acceptable in School or College. There are some idiosyncratic spellings: 'owne' for 'own', what appears to be 'charing' for 'charge', 'slave' for 'self' and 'wont' for 'what'. Some punctuation should also be inserted before 'you tell . . .'

Similar points can be made all the way through. It is seldom difficult to see what she means. The meaning of '. . . . but I think it is too much independance of yourself' is not readily available, nor that carried by the last seven words. They reflect her difficulties in combining words into meaning-carrying structures, just as she sometimes has difficulty in combining letters into words.

How—apart from not giving her tasks that lie too far outside the range of her meaning potential—can she be helped? Only if she is encouraged to exploit the resources she already has.

She displays a promising grasp of fairly complex structures. She can begin, 'If you are having a place of your (own) . . .'

74

and continue, 'windows should be (displayed) nicely.' Something
went wrong in the middle, so that she wrote, 'a place of your
windows' instead of, presumably, 'a place of your own, your
windows. . . .' But the underlying sentence structure is clearly
discernible, as it is in 'before I (start) a business I would have to
have (lots of) money and (people) to help me start my business.'
There is evidence here of potential literacy. The language is
there.

Her spelling, too, displays evidence of what she knows and what
she can do. In some instances, as in 'slave' for 'self' and 'wont' for
'what' she has attempted a correspondence between sound and
symbol that at least has a discernible relationship. She occasionally adds a letter ('owne' for 'own') or misses one out ('pople' for
'people') or transposes two ('hlep' for 'help'). She can put in too
many syllables ('independependance'), and she can get in a tangle
with 'despeldy' for 'displayed', or when she runs off the page in
the last line but one with what looks as if it might have been
'hairdressers', and with the word under that, which is the only
*word* in the piece which causes insuperable difficulty to the reader.
But if what she (or anyone else) writes is regarded as evidence of
*knowledge*, and hence of resource, or potential, instead of evidence
of ignorance, then ways can be devised of helping her to capitalise
on what she possesses.[17]

Using criteria like this, what could be said about the following?

(a) I am very sorry, that I made plenty noise in your class, and I
know that is my foult. And I am asking that I would not do it
any more to upset you and I am very sorry for that is because I
mist a fall on the ground. And I want to get on with my typing
so I am asking you if you would correct my work please and I
promise that I would not go back in your book any more, please
I am very sorry.

(b) Dear Sir,
I would like you to bring a hearse and a coffin for my beloved
friend P. Rees who passed away on the 21st April in a terrible
car accident in which he was split in two and serious head injuries.
I am happy to say that he died instantly and felt no pain whatever.
I would like the deceased to have a silk lined coffin with brass
handles on the side, and I would like the hearse to be one of your
best. Please collect the body on the 23rd April from my flat.

To service a Motor cycle.

Plenty of rags the more the better, chrome cleaner, "gunk", spanners, screwdrivers, buckets of warm soapy water and most important of all plenty, and I mean plenty, of patients are just a few of the things needed when starting such a hard task Time seems to float past when you are cleaning every nut and bolt holding the motor cycle together. It could take as long as a week to make a real profession -al job A rusty much rotten heap transformed into a glemming machine to be proud off A dream that seems further away the longer you work

The bike in question a Honda 175cc CB 'K' registration, new maybe but it get rusty all the same

Spanner to the attension, dismantly the main parts leave only the frame engine and wheels Spanner one , ten millimeter, remove the two nut locating the exhaust to the cylinder head, no technical names for the simple reason I don't know them myself. Twelve millimeter spanner, holding the exhaust to the frame are two nuts which can be found easily and removed away comes The whole exhaust unit with a gentle push forward to free the exhaust from the cylinder head keep the nuts and washers in a safe place tempers are roubed by missing pieces. Repeat for the second exhaust

The tank will have to come off, bad luck if there is any petrol inside a nessey operation. Switch the petrol tap off remove the two rubber tube leading from the tank to the twin carburators. The tube connecting one half of the tank to the other is the most difficult petrol pours out have a tin can ready disconnect the tube and let the liquid flow into the 'can' a welcome job, the tank will now lift off

## Language study for teachers

How can pupils and students who produce pieces of writing like this be put into a position in which they can develop the language and language experience that they have got, instead of constantly being put into positions in which they will, inevitably, be condemned for not possessing knowledge and experience they haven't got?

The answer must be, only when their teachers have an adequate and relevant knowledge of the nature and function of language, especially as it plays its part in the learning process.

What is meant here by relevant is described by Dell Hymes, in his Introduction to *Functions of Language in the Classroom*, like this:

'What is crucial is not so much a better understanding of how language is structured, but a better understanding of how language is used; not so much what language is, as what language is for . . . what we need to know goes far beyond how the grammar of English is organized as something to be taught. It has to do with the relationship between a grammar of English and the ways in which English is organized in use by teachers, by children and by the communities from which they come; with the features of intonation, tone of voice, rhythm, style, that escape the usual grammar and enter into the essential meaning of speech; with the meanings of all those means of speech to those who use them and those who hear them, not in the narrow sense of meaning, as in naming objects and stating relationships, but in the fuller sense, as conveying respect or disrespect, concern or indifference, intimacy or distance, seriousness or play, etc; with the appropriateness of one or another means of speech, or way of speaking, to one or another topic, person, situation; in short, with the relation of the structure of language to the structure of speaking.'

Equipped with this kind of understanding, teachers would be better placed to discern potential, better placed to devise learning situations in which pupils can develop their potential.

It is part of the argument of this book that this will entail looking at, and where necessary altering, ways in which schools are organised. It entails examining ways in which all subjects are taught, or, in the terms of the way in which the process has been seen in this book, examining opportunities given to pupils to meet the language demands of this subject or that.

It means, quite certainly, looking again at techniques of assessment and marking, by asking questions like,

'For whose sake are we assessing?'

'What is the point of marking?'

'How will marking help the pupil to perform more adequately next time?'

'Are "errors" and "mistakes" to be regarded as evidence of knowledge, and hence of potential, or as some kind of linguistic sin?'

It entails nothing less than placing at the service of the pupils, in learning situations that the school sets up, all that we can discover about the way in which language actually works that will help them to succeed. In this way we might change a situation in which everything seems to conspire against certain pupils—those pupils whose language is under-valued; those pupils who have had less experience of the kind of language on which the school puts a premium; pupils who are accorded low status in relationships set up ostensibly to promote learning; pupils constantly devalued by the whole apparatus of evaluation; in short, pupils whose efforts are seen, 'at best, as irrelevant to the educational endeavour'.

# References

1 (p. 13) Reprinted in Bernstein, B. (ed.), *Class, Codes and Control*, Vol. 1. Theoretical Studies towards a Sociology of Language (Routledge & Kegan Paul).

2 (p. 13) Halliday, M. A. K., *Language and social man* (Papers in Linguistics and English Teaching, series 11, Longman). See also *Learning How To Mean* in this series (Edward Arnold).

3 (p. 13) Hasan, R., 'Code, register and social dialect', in Bernstein, B. (ed.), *Class, Codes and Control*, Vol. 11, Applied Studies towards a Sociology of Language (Routledge & Kegan Paul).

4 (p. 17) Doughty, E. A. and P. S., *Language and Community* in this series (Edward Arnold).

5 (p. 19) Doughty, P. S., Pearce, J. J. and Thornton, G. M., *Exploring Language*, Chapter 1 (Edward Arnold).

6 (p. 20) Byers, P. and H., 'Nonverbal Communication and the Education of Children', in Cazden C., John V. P. and Dell Hymes (ed.), *Functions of Language in the Classroom* (Teachers College Press).

7 (p. 24) Fader, D., *Hooked on Books* (Pergamon Press).

8 (p. 35) Berger, P. L. and Luckmann, T. *The Social Construction of Reality* (Penguin)

9 (p. 38) Gurney, R., *Language, Brain and Interactive Processes*, in this series (Edward Arnold).

10 (p. 44) Labov, W., 'The logic of Non-standard English' in Keddie, N. (ed), *Tinker, Tailor* (Penguin). See also Torrey, J., 'Illiteracy in the Ghetto' in the same volume.

11 (p. 47) Abercrombie, D., 'R.P. and Local Accent' in *Studies in Phonetics and Linguistics* (O.U.P.)

12 (p. 55) Joos, M., *The Five Clocks* (Harcourt Brace).
13 (p. 64) Barnes, D., *Language in the Classroom* (Open University Correspondence Text).
*From Communication to Curriculum* (Penguin).
14 (p. 65) Doughty, P., Pearce, J. J. and Thornton, G. M., *Language in Use* (Edward Arnold).
See also Doughty, E. A. and P.S. *Using 'Language in Use': a teacher's guide to language work in the classroom* (Edward Arnold)
15 (p. 65) McIntosh, A. 'Language and Style', in Pride, J. B., Holmes, J. (ed.), *Sociolinguistics* (Penguin).
16 (p. 67) Hasan, R., 'Grammatical cohesion in spoken and written English, part one' (Papers in Linguistics and English Teaching, Series 1, Longman).
17 (p. 75) See, in this connection, Albrow, K. H., *The English writing system: notes towards a description* (Papers in Linguistics and English Teaching, Series 11, Longman).